I0671527

The Road Less Traveled

Published by

6500 Clito Road
Statesboro, Georgia 30467 (USA)

© 2010 by Charles E. Cravey
ALL RIGHTS RESERVED!

All Scripture References are from the King James Version
of the Holy Bible (KJV) unless otherwise noted.

Printed in the United States of America
Published by IN HIS STEPS PUBLISHING
Statesboro, Georgia 30461

ISBN: 1-58535-189-X

The Road Less Traveled

Charles E. Cravey

In His Steps Publishing

"He answered and said,
Whether he be a sinner or no,
I know not:
one thing I know, that,
whereas I was blind, now I see."

John 9:25

Contents

Introduction

Let me make this perfectly clear from the onset: I am NOT a great writer. I work very diligently at sentence structure and story lines and have to rely upon my good friends to help proofread and give constructive criticism along the way. Patsy DeLoach and Renee Cravey, both teachers of many years, constantly remind me that I'm wild about putting too many commas in my sentences, as well as semi-colons. I must admit that on those days in school when we were instructed in English class on how to apply such to our writing, I was sitting over in the corner daydreaming as I looked out the window to the world beyond. That's where I wanted to be—in the REAL world! Renee and Patsy have taught me a lot, but you are sure to find more than just commas and semi-colons and exclamation points in these writings. Patsy tells me that I abuse the use of exclamation points in just about every sentence. She's right because I think that everything in this world deserves an exclamation! It is just that precious and special to me.

This book is my attempt at putting an exclamation point to my life. I have traveled widely across the world and have experienced more in a few years than most people do in a lifetime. I wanted to share some of those experiences with you and how I've learned some very important life-lessons along the way. If my writings touch one other soul then my work has been worth it all.

May you find something in these pages that you have been looking for. It is my fervent prayer that you may also begin to put more exclamation points in YOUR life as I have in mine. To God be the glory and honor for it all, for without Him, this would not have been possible.

I love the countryside and the beauty and simplicity it offers to the viewer. There I find my bearings in life when things become so hectic and busy.

The Road Less Traveled is my proclamation to the world that I have taken a different path in life than most. I have looked down each path longingly and have chosen the one you are about to embark upon now in this book.

Blessed be your journey, my friend!

Charles E. Cravey
December 2010

"Justification"

Do you remember the age at which you felt actually smarter than your parents? Do you also remember your first rebellion against their authority, and the ultimate consequences of your rebellious act of disobedience? I'd rather not personally say what my punishment was, but I'm almost certain we've all had those challenges growing up.

In Genesis chapter twelve, God gives a command to Abram to pack up his personal belongings for a journey. Furthermore, he is to carry only Sarah, his wife, and Lot, his nephew, with him. God was calling Abram to move to the land of Canaan, an unknown land to Abram at that time. Now get this, Abram was 75 years old! When most of his contemporaries were living lives retired in Panama City or Cancun, taking it easy, Abram had to begin all over again! Imagine how he must have felt. I don't know about you, but I would have felt a good bit hesitant to say "yes" to such a command, but not Abram. He was ready for the challenge and so must we be ready and obedient whenever our Lord calls.

As I write this discourse, it is the second Sunday in the 40 day period of Lent which leads to Easter. It is a time in which we are called to give up something in our lives in order to fully concentrate and grow closer to Christ. I wonder how many people are actually giving up things that hinder their spiritual journeys? What have you given up thus far? Could not part of our faithfulness to God be encapsulated in our willingness to give up those things which separate us from God's Grace? If we are uncertain as to God's Call upon our lives, perhaps it is because we have not cleared our agendas for His! Many times we are often too "busy" to hear God's call.

Abram's story carries both a **precept** and a **promise**. It is a testing precept of leaving the comfort-creature lifestyles he has come to know, and taking off completely in faith to a strange land that God is to show him. In this, Abram understands that his natural affections must give way to divine grace. Sin must be forsaken. He must abandon all idols, willingly departing with only those things nearest and dearest to him.

God then promises Abram six things if he will be obedient to His call:

(1) I will make you into a great nation.

(2) I will bless you.

(3) I will make your name great. Abram lost his old name in the process and received the new name of *Abra-*

ham.

(4) You will be a blessing.

(5) I will bless those who bless you and curse those who curse you.

(6) All people on earth will be blessed through you.

In reality, would *we* go? At God's command, would we be obedient to leave the comforts of home and family and move to another country, another state, another place in our existence? We will never find our true rest until we answer God's call through faithfulness. God desires each of us to have intimate fellowship with Him and to trust Him completely. In order to do this, we must lose ourselves and gain Christ!

Let's look at Psalm 121. In this chapter we have that beautiful passage from David reminding us that the Lord will bless us and keep us in all ways if we are obedient to His call. He will bless our "going out" and our "coming in." David said, "My help cometh from the Lord." David calls us to have confidence in God and trust in His holy ways. Do we put our faith and trust in mountains, in powers, in people? No! Our only help is in the Lord. He will keep us.

In Romans 4:1-5 and 13-17, we have Paul's explanation of **justification by faith**, one of our major church doctrines. Paul even uses Abraham here as an example, stating that Abraham *believed in God and it was reckoned to him as righteousness*. The Jews believed firmly in the Laws of God, but rejected Paul's teachings of faith alone. Paul would note later that faith would be followed by action and in the keeping of the Law. The promises came to Abraham by faith and not by the law. The promise rests solely upon grace.

In John 3:1-17, we have the Pharisee Nicodemus, a devout leader of the Jews and a member of the Sanhedrin, coming to Jesus at night with questions. He recognized Jesus immediately as a "Rabbi" (teacher) who knew the Law and desired to know more from this teacher.

Nicodemus asks how it is possible for a person to be born again; how could one re-enter his mother's womb a second time? Jesus responds with these words, "What is born of the flesh is flesh, and what is born of the Spirit is spirit."

It was apparent that Nicodemus could not look beyond the Old Testament laws and spiritually discern what Jesus was advocating because he was blinded to all spiritual matters by his belief in "works."

Jesus then presents the plan of salvation to Nicodemus in verse 16 - "For God so loved the world that he gave his only begotten son that whosoever believeth in him should not perish but have everlasting life." This had to be too simple for Nicodemus to accept, and so he walked away from the presence of Jesus.

Here's the message in a nutshell:

(1) God is calling new Abrahams into the world.

(2) God promises to bless our obedience.

(3) We have the assurance of His protection at all times.

(4) We are justified by our faith in Jesus Christ by believing in him personally and answering His call.

(5) Finally, we must be born again by water and the Spirit.

"When we walk with the Lord, in the light of His Word,
What a glory he sheds on our way.
While we do his good will, he abides with us still,
And with all who will trust and obey!"

"Trust and obey, for there's no other way
To be happy in Jesus, but to Trust and Obey."

(From the hymn—"Trust and Obey" - written by
John H. Sammis, 1887)

If you hear the voice of God calling you forth today, let me invite you to His throne of Grace. If you sense that your faith is not as strong as you desire it to be, then come and lay down that "something" in your life that may be separating you from a deeper, more abiding faith. If you are spiritually hungry, come and be fed. If you desire to begin living a new life, then step out in faith and give your heart completely to Christ. Leave the law behind and be justified by your faith in Almighty God. The invitation is given. Come.

I Saw God in the Muck-and-Mire

I saw God walking on Lake Pontchartrain;
Another miracle in the making after Katrina.
He stood in the doorway of a devastated
and flooded home,
And waved to those who passed by
but could not see.
They were not looking for Him.
I saw Him tenderly caress a broken lady who toured
her home for the first time in three months and saw it
in complete ruin.
He reached out and touched her heart through volunteers
piling out of a church van to help clean up her home;
simple people of faith who really cared
and did what they could in such turmoil.
Her tears expressed the acknowledgement of
God's presence.
Five-feet high the water came
as it rose from the broken levees and
flooded her home, destroying a lifetime of memories.
Her hurt was real and God's heart was broken;
another cross to bear,
a heart to mend,
a world to reconcile.
I saw God through it all
and took His hand as we walked together
through the muck-and-mire of life's broken dreams.
"There but for the grace of God . . ."

(Written following my first of six mission trips to New Orleans, Louisiana, to help in the cleanup operations following Hurricane Katrina.)

Closed—Until Further Notice

Emotions run deep, and adrenalin surges through my mind as I stand gazing upon what once was. Flickers from the past rush by as I imagine the activities that once permeated this vacant structure, now consumed by time. Vines fill the void where life once existed; people coming and going, business as usual, smiling faces transacting deals and bargains.

Any signs of life have long since departed from this solitary structure; only the elements of nature have taken their toll. What once exuded a vibrant life has now been relegated to crumbling brick, weakened mortar, sand and stone. If only these walls could talk, what stories of a bygone era would they tell? And yet, when these doors were closed and locked for the very last time and its owner stood here remembering its history, certainly a tear had to appear as he wept over the structure before him.

Closed—until further notice. Perhaps there were no intentions of ever returning. Can we go back to things as they were in the past? Circumstances and people change and directions are re-chartered. We move on—down that path of least resistance, to some uncertain future, carrying our baggage of memories in tow, while the past is consumed by elements of time.

When I left home and married my wife and married my job, I somehow knew that I would never return again to things as they were. That part of my past had closed, and so I moved on, choosing the future as a lover, grabbing hold of what it offered, and setting my course for eternity. I've often taken the *"road less traveled"* and it has made all the difference in my life.

And so I've poured myself into the past thirty-eight years of life and ministry. I've been met with joy and happiness, sorrow and pain, and a world of constant change. When I first set out on my journey, life seemed so simple but it quickly became confusing and difficult. I was not given a handbook or a roadmap—simply choices and paths before me. I, and I alone, would have to make those difficult choices and decide which paths to travel.

At this juncture in my life, I've been met with the recent passing of my mother, her strength sapped from her by a life-ending stroke. The strongest person I've ever known was reduced to an invalid in a nursing home bed in her last days. She was the stalwart in my life, ever reminding me that I had to push forward and never look back, reminding me that I could visit home again but it would never be the same.

I also lost a dear brother at a young age. My father died when I was fifteen. I've stood beside the bed of numerous dying church members and have watched, in those waning moments, how death comes and takes us away, sometimes quietly and, at others, violently. Death is final; the door has been closed; the path has come to an end. Closed—until further notice.

Would that we could return to that simple and uncomplicated past when we sat on daddy's lap and played games all day with the neighborhood children. Yet, that life, as endless as it seemed at the time, has been taken over with the vines of time.

Just today I stood in front of a vacant lot on Pot-Liquor Hill where our old clap-boarded house once stood. I could still visualize it in my mind's eye; but it was physically destroyed years ago. I stood there and remembered some of the precious events of my formative life. Cobwebs of the mind now cloud some of my thoughts.

Mama, daddy and brother are now resting in Little Rock Cemetery. Their graves are cold and covered with stone, but their memories linger. I cannot bring them back. I cannot return home again.

These next few days, weeks and months will determine my destiny as I seek a new path, a new vision, a new direction for the rest of my life. My past has been "closed—until further notice." And so, I pack up my little red wagon and, once again, move confidently into that vague and uncertain future, knowing there is yet a lot of life to live at fifty-nine before the sands of time and the elements of nature place me beneath a cold, hard stone.

The sun glistens on the old building as I stand looking. Late afternoon. Wind softly blows the ivy as I shed a tear for what once was.

Happy Birthday, America!

Cluttered beneath the remnants of long, hot, sultry days of childhood, lay the embossed feelings and emotions, latent now from the responsibilities of adulthood. Somewhere deep, under the archives of the past, are those events and experiences which eventually mold and shape one's life.

I remember my dad in faded khakis, stumbling home down a single-lane dirt road. It seemed then that dad was always trying to find his way back home. In such inebriated states, he would often recall Pearl Harbor, Iwo Jima, Midway and the young men he had shot and killed on foreign shores for our freedom. Dad never forgot those painful and traumatic days of trudging through the muck-and-mire of a newly discovered world, finding it entirely different from his country-boy childhood. Innocence lost— confronting death on a daily basis—nearly freezing to death in bunker after bunker—with all the ghosts of the past now preying on his soul as a stalker preys upon its subject. Demons haunted him daily.

I remember dad's tears of remorse. He could never quite seem to return to the simple plow-boy of his youth. They were now gone, ripped from him like a razor, severed and scattered through the years in a cruel and precise act called maturity.

As I stand at the foot of his simple slab grave in this sand-ridge cemetery, I am transported briefly back to early memories of those days on our front porch, a respite from our work in the fields. There, I recall dad sitting me upon his knee, strong-armed and able, as he would begin to rock me in complete silence—as though when sober he became mute, unable to talk about it—the war—that part of his life he had tried over and again to box-up and leave somewhere under the clutter of the past. That's the part I remember best about dad. All other things are now lost forever. I was fifteen when he died.

I remember the twenty-one-gun salute, taps (which made me cry), and the solemnity of that hot, summer day when we laid my dad to rest. Rest? Was he finally "at rest" from the demons who constantly pursued him?

They folded an American flag at his grave and gave it to my mom. She clasped it and offered her tears for the many years of father's pain. Somewhere, folded into the flaps of that flag, interwoven in the very fabric, pieced together in the embroidered stars, are my memories of dad and childhood. That flag symbolizes who I am and who my father was, and the countless others who fought and gave more than blood and guts upon battlefields across the world; they gave their innocence! Some of us still remember. Happy birthday, America!

Friendship

The phone rang and on the other end was my dear friend and colleague, Don Combs, calling to express his concerns about me. I had recently been through a certain dilemma in my life, and he had received news of it. He expressed true attributes of friendship by reaching out to me with sympathy and understanding. Our conversation never once turned to himself, but was all about me and my situation. His appeal to help, in any possible way, was like a breath of fresh air. By lifting my spirits, Don gave me renewed strength and courage to continue fighting my battle.

There were others who called with similar concern. Another friend and colleague, Terry DeLoach, called to let me know that he and his wife, Patsy, were behind me 100% and whatever I needed they would try to provide.

And then there was Hugh Hunter who lifted my spirits by emailing me and offering his assistance in any way possible. He is a true friend in every aspect.

How can a person possibly survive without friends? John Donne once stated that " . . . no man is an island . . ." How true. We are all part and parcel of one another in the larger scheme of things. Thank God for friendship!

Bobby McDaniel Eulogy

Glenwood, GA - 7/25/09

Ecclesiastes 3:11 states that *"God has planted eternity in the human heart."*

In the beautiful trilogy "Lord of the Rings," two little hobbits, Sam and Frodo are sent off into an evil world to save it. Calamities happen to them; they escape many encounters by the hair on their heads; the dark world has a hold on them, but they are determined to press forward to their higher calling. At one desperate point in the saga, Sam turns to Frodo and says, *"I wonder what sort of tale we've fallen into."*

Isn't that life? Isn't that our question as well? Ours is a story yet to be told.

I remember those beautiful lines from an innocent Forrest Gump when he stands beside his dying mother's bed and asks her the question: *"Mama, what's my destiny?"* Her response was those now famous words, *"Forrest, life is like a box of chocolates; you never know what you're gonna get."*

And so it is with Life. We never know what the next bend in the road will bring, but we, like Sam and Frodo, keep pressing on, deeper and deeper into this life and its circumstances, doing our best to find our destiny, our place in the overall scheme of things. But there is One much greater Who knows the entire story of our lives and has promised never to leave us or forsake us in our hour of trial but would, in all ways prepare a means of escape for us, even in our darkest hour.

I firmly believe that our Savior came on Wednesday night to receive our dear brother, Bobby. There was nothing that any of us could have done to have changed that. Those final days of his life were to prepare us for the journey that took place in that hospice room. The saga of his earthly life came to a close, opening that beautiful realm of God's heaven to a much deserved pilgrim who is now HOME.

Where will the saga of our lives take us? What events will transpire to shape us into the persons God is calling us to be? It has yet to be determined how we will live out the remaining days and years of our lives, but He Who holds the keys to life and death will stand with us and never leave us. HE will be our shield and our defender and will maintain His promise of eternity with Him if we are faithful, for *"He has planted eternity in the human heart."*

Why Am I So Empty?

Emptiness. The word implies the total lack of substance. I've heard the statement, often implied of a person who has lost everything, that "he's just a shell of a man." What does that mean? Does it mean he's only flesh and blood without a soul? Or does it mean he no longer has a reason to live? Emptiness—the absence of substance.

In man's quest to know more about the universe in which we live, billions of dollars are invested annually in our search for and quest of a better life. Why? Why do we do what we do? We want to know how to fill the great void in our lives. The universe and planets beyond our reach will never fulfill the needs we require. With billions spent in our space program alone, are we any closer to discovering God?

Let me share an important word with you right now: **We are empty because there is a God-shaped hole in our hearts that only HE can fill!** And so we explore the universe, our own little world, read books, research constantly--all in an attempt to fill that void.

Companies today have what are called **"THINK TANKS"** in which workers gather around tables all day and do nothing but THINK. How would you like to get paid to do nothing but THINK? Companies have found invaluable such groups who can often see things from a different perspective.

In our daily lives we keep a calendar. I couldn't really function without one. I have to mark down all of my appointments and keep a very strict schedule most days of the week. We are always searching for ways to streamline our lives and to simplify daily living.

But what about the greater issues of life and death? Do we plan? Do we need to search for answers to the deep moral and spiritual questions so that our lives are more orderly? That's why we have philosophers, psychologists and theologians, right?

We want to know why we are so empty when we seem to have so much! The oldest book in the possession of the human race is JOB, and Job once exclaimed, *"Oh, that I knew where I might find Him (God)"* **(Job 23:3)**. This search transcends race, age, economic status, sex, and educational background. Either man began nowhere and is looking for some place to go, or he began somewhere and lost his way. In either case, he's searching. None of us will ever find "total satisfaction" until we find that our roots are in eternity!

We all want to know how to fill the God-shaped void in our souls. There are empty souls all around us. Chuck Colson of Watergate fame, was quoted once as saying, *"All the material things in life are meaningless if a man hasn't discovered what's underneath them . . ."* All of the "stuff" in our lives will not satisfy nor fill that empty void; only GOD CAN!

Think about this scripture from **Luke 12:15:** *"Not even when one has an abundance does his life consist of his possessions."* Think about that. We came into this world naked and we will leave it in similar fashion. We cannot take any possessions with us. Therefore, what matters the most in life? If you had one more month to live, how would you spend it? Would you fill it with "things" that really don't matter? Or would you seek to fill it with *that* which will eternally satisfy your soul--the THINGS OF GOD?

I was eighteen when I gave my heart to Jesus and filled that empty void. That was the greatest moment in my life. I realized for the first time that someone else was in charge of my life and that my life now belonged to Him.

When I decided to give up my "stuff" (possessions) and turn it all over to Christ, the void in me became filled with the grace and glory of God! How awesome that was! The sweetness of Christ entering into my heart will always be the most glorious day of my life. Nothing since has compared to that moment of salvation when I came to know God and to understand that He accepted me with all of my blemishes, my sin and my pain. I didn't have to search any longer, for now He was dwelling within that void, completely filling it with His wonderful love, mercy and grace.

I want to challenge each of you to give up your "stuff," your possessions, and offer them to God in exchange for that sweetness and peace that the world just cannot give you. I want you to make that decision to know Christ in His infinite goodness and invite Him into your heart.

I know, you still don't have all the answers to the mysteries of life, and may never have, but you'll be on your way to learning more about the God who created you in His own image and likeness.

Prophecy

As I write this, America is involved in two major wars in the Middle East; world economics seem to be falling apart; our oldest and most reliable institutions are crumbling; churches are fighting internally and threatening the very faith of our people. Sex is shown over the internet and TV openly. Children are rising up and slaying their parents in the streets . . .

I am drawn to the Revelation of John who predicted such things occurring. It was two-thousand years ago that he predicted these things happening prior to the second-coming of Christ. Could we be in those latter days? Can we put Pandora safely back in her box without further damage being done? Can we turn this thing around before it's too late? Will people care enough about the severity of the situation to do anything about it? Where are our convictions when our morals are crumbling around us?

I am not a prophet of doom, but a mere observer of the world around me. I've traveled it extensively and it doesn't take a rocket scientist to realize that our planet is near self-destruction. When the reality of global warming is the leading discussion on the pages of our newspapers, one has to believe that we're in danger.

The great golfer, Tiger Woods, has just admitted to immorality and his wife is seeking a divorce and settlement. He was a great role model for our youth, but now that image has been tarnished, perhaps beyond recovery. Our children hunger for someone to lead them and in whom they can put their trust. We're adrift on an endless sea of apathy which consumes our heart and soul. Who will right the ship and steer us in the direction we need to go?

In 1970, I remember attending a David Wilkerson Crusade at the Macon Coliseum and listening to his dim views of the future. His new book (at that time), entitled *The Vision*, was hot off the presses and folks were flocking to hear his God-given predictions of the future. My friends and I discussed those predictions on our drive home, and most of us felt "No Way!" would or could those things happen. And now, 2010, I've returned to his little volume to find his predictions are true.

America has lost its heart and soul and *must* return to faith in God in order to survive these troubling times. Evil lurks about us, but instead of overcoming it by our faith in Christ, we are compromising with it. This becomes a broad road that leads to destruction. May we choose the narrow road and faith to help restore our nation before it's too late. Pray with me and others today, and then put your prayers and faith into action. Time is now of the essence!

Saga

I only wish I had been there in the beginning—before the worlds were formed—before evil entered our lives—before . . . And yet, I was not. As John Eldredge implies in *Epic*, I was dropped midstream into this saga, this story of stories, to find my way through the maze and to discover my place in a world where the story has already evolved to this extent.

I did not choose my parents, the home I grew up in, the schools I attended, or the folks who surrounded me. I had no choice in the chain of events that occurred prior to my birth. I was simply given birth by an eighth grade drop-out who had to struggle to make ends meet and to put food on our table for three hungry sharecropper boys. Life was hard and her circumstances made it even harder. Mama's dreams were quickly shattered early in her life, and she had to change course and work her fingers to the bone simply to survive. Dreams of learning music, going to Nashville, becoming a gospel singer all changed when she became pregnant with her first child.

My father, a sharecropper, had to leave school early in his elementary grades to help out on the farm. He never went back and eventually signed with the Army to join the cause at the on set of World War II. His life would dramatically change through that experience of war, death and the aftermath. He took to the bottle to help ease his inner pain. His death came when I was fifteen, and it made things even tougher for our family, causing my mom to secure a second job just to pay the bills. Times were hard and I had no control over many of these events which helped to shape my formative years. The saga was already set into motion when I arrived. I was dropped into the midst of it all and left here without a guide book.

I would have changed it all had I been given a choice. I would have created a world where pain, hurt and suffering did not exist, where everyone lived in complete harmony; where nothing had to die in a meaningless fashion. It would have been a perfect environment, beautiful beyond measure, and filled with peace, joy and love. But I wasn't given that choice. I became part of a world already in turmoil, a world filled with mixed emotions, a story already being told with each act coming before and after me.

Where was *my* place in the scheme of things? What was *my* purpose in all of it? This question plagued me as a young man and I would constantly sit under my favorite old oak tree and contemplate the meaning of it all.

What is *our* destiny? Where do *we* fit into the scheme of things? We spend our lives, therefore, watching things fall into place which ultimately defines our purpose and destiny. It doesn't happen over night, even though our impatience wants to know "right now!" It is wrought by the accumulation of many events throughout a lifetime and the resulting discoveries.

Each event of my life, though unforeseen or imagined at the time, formed the person I have become today. Those events could have ended differently and changed my destiny. It all depends upon how I enter such events and how I deal with them once they occur.

I continue on my journey (destiny) daily, taking various roads before me, knowing that any potential choice could greatly affect the rest of my life. I must move forward with all the confidence I can muster, carefully choosing which roads I will take. Knowing my very nature, I am prone to take some roads, like Robert Frost's *The Road Not Taken*, for I've always been the inquisitive type, wanting to know what is down that narrow path which few travel. Some of my most blessed moments have come from taking such paths.

Where will your paths lead? I trust and pray that they
will lead you home.

Country Boy

I remember those early mornings back in the 1960s when I would be awakened at five a.m. for work. After picking up other workers for the day, we would make our way to the fields of cotton, corn, cucumbers, watermelons, cantaloupes, peas and beans, okra and various other truck crops. Croaker sack or bushel basket in hand, we would start at the beginning of endless rows of produce, usually drenched by the early morning dew. We would fill our sacks or baskets and return to the tractor to unload. Over and over throughout the day, we would repeat this process until our 8-10 hour day had ended. We would then jump on the back of trucks for our ride home where we would still be responsible for helping out around the house. With no TV set, we would first sit around the kitchen table and eat mama's delicious supper, then clean the dishes, bathe, and sit around a little while and listen to the radio, read books, or make small talk until bedtime, which usually came around 8-9 p.m.

Back then, without a bathroom in the house, we would take sponge-baths in the kitchen sink after return- ing home from work. Saturday was the BIG bath day. Mama would fill up a #10 tub with hot water heated on our old pot-bellied stove. It would be mixed with cold water from the backyard spigot. One-by-one we would take our turn in the tub, often with nothing more than underwear on! Winters would find us taking mostly sponge baths due to the extreme cold outside.

I remember city kids laughing at and taunting us when we went to school. We talked a bit different, had holey clothes and well-worn shoes, handed down to us by neighbors or our next elder sibling. It was often embarrassing to be picked on, but country boys still have their pride and so we were often involved in fights to defend our honor at school. I usually frequented the principal's office due to such fights, but would never once back down!

Most of our toys were gleaned from the city dump, located a couple of miles from our home. We learned how to take the discarded toys of others and repair them for further use. My first bicycle was formed from various tires, nuts and bolts, and frames from the dump. We learned how to patch inner-tubes and keep the bikes rolling.

Go carts were our favorite form of play, and these would be put together from objects found at the dump. As a six-year-old, a simple brick would give me hours of pleasure in the fields around our home place. It would become my car or truck, and I would use it to make roads in the dirt fields around our house. My imagination took me to many exotic and foreign places that I had only heard about at school through books. My imaginary friend, *Leroy*, traveled with me and kept me company in those early years. Guess I was around nine or ten when friends at school took Leroy's place in my life, and I seemed to forget about him, although I knew he never existed!

Sundays found us down at either Sugar Creek or the Whirl-Hole swimming or fishing. I remember nearly drowning on four separate occasions, but, luckily, someone would always pull me to safety just in time! It is ironic that, many years later, my oldest brother, Raymond, who had saved me on a couple of those occasions, would actually drown in that Whirl-Hole saving a mother and her three-year-old daughter! I tremble each time I remember his unselfishness and constant care for others. He was very first "hero" and will always be held in high-esteem in my heart.

We played stick-baseball back then. We never had access to a "real" baseball or bat until I began playing Little League baseball. Our bats were usually old dried limbs from one of the oak trees surrounding our property, cut down to size, or we would use a stick of lumber from daddy's woodpile. Our ball would often be a rock or heavy object wound by cloth to ball size and tied off with string. We played in open fields or sandlots and gathered neighboring kids each day to join us as we competed against each other. We usually played in bare feet and would occasionally pick up splinters or briars or would step on cut glass and collect a gash, but we played on!

When I was old enough for Little League, I had my first taste of real baseballs, bats and gloves. What a difference they made! My life began to evolve around baseball from that moment on. When asked by my coach, in my second game, to catch behind the plate, I gladly accepted and learned to love that position, which I would play exclusively over my baseball career.

I remember the first team uniform. It was bright green trimmed suit with green stockings which had three white stripes on them. That was the first new set of clothes I had ever worn, and I felt so important and took great pride, wearing it for our sponsor—Walker Concrete Pipe Company. Those were good days in which I was always immediately picked as the #1 All-Star Catcher year after year. I treasured each of those precious moments back then.

Today, following surgery on both knees, repairing the vertebrae in my neck, suffering a bad lower back and facing surgery on my right foot following a church-league softball game (at age fifty-eight!), I guess that I am paying the consequences of my many years of catching, but I would not take away those great days of my past for anything.

My mother was the master of disguises when cooking. She could somehow make a slice of bologna taste like steak! She was a great cook and actually worked at my elementary school lunchroom during the day and at a local restaurant as a cook at night. God rest her soul, that lady more than earned her rest in the Lord! She was a magician with food preparation.

Back then, our shirts and pants were all made by mama. Shirts were made from flour sacks. Mama was a master seamstress and could turn any kind of cloth into a true work of art. Country folk learn to make do with what they have. I remember mama quilting using scraps of material given to her by neighbors and friends. Those quilts kept us warm and comfortable through the hard winters. One of my most prized possessions today is a quilt that mama gave to my wife and me when we were married. That was her special contribution to our marriage, and a welcomed and useful one.

Country folk know how to survive and often flourish when others seem to fail. Having grown up with that kind of heritage has made me a much stronger person, more caring, more entrepreneurial, and with a greater drive to survive. *"I thank God I'm a Country Boy!"*

Attitude and Recovery

What do you do when you encounter the worst day of your life? The answer to that rests solely upon attitude. Faith is that substance which drives our attitude. Dependent upon *what* or *whom* you believe in, your faith and trust in that element will drive you to recovery or disaster. Dependent upon that attitude, your life and dilemma can either become a blessing or a curse.

Let me share a biblical story that will enforce this premise. The story of David is a prime study. About a thousand years prior to the birth of Christ, David was in command of King Saul's armies. He had been very successful and his troops had won many victories in battle. His esteem was very high, and his people had elevated him to "hero" status. This is the same David who had slain the giant, Goliath, in the Valley of Elah some years prior when David was a teenager.

David and his family were living in Ziklag. Following a three-day journey from Ziklag, David and his army returned home to find everything in utter ruin. Their city had been set ablaze and their animals, women and children taken hostage by the Amalekites.

David and his army could have fallen to their knees in

the midst of their calamity and allowed depression to set in. They could have easily cried out, "Woe is me!," but David's faith in the almighty God would not allow him to tarry long in the depths of their grief and despair. God leads them into battle against their arch rivals, the Amalekites. In the process, David and his army destroyed and ran off a remnant of the Amalekites and recovered what was rightfully theirs. In fact, they recovered the spoils left behind by the Amalekites and took much more home with them than they had originally lost! David and his army recovered through David's faithfulness to God.

It is our faith which ultimately enables our recovery, even in the midst of the worst experiences of our lives. You can and will make it if you allow God to help. Do not allow self-pity to invade your mind and destroy your hope. You are simply going through a valley, somewhere between where you've been in life and where God wants you to be. God did not necessarily bring you to this valley but will make a way of escape to those who put their faith and trust in Him. Hope in God will eventually turn our sorrow into joy. We *must not* give up and allow Satan to destroy us. We must keep a proper perspective on what is occurring in our lives and rise above it all and move towards recovery. With patience in God and faith in His almighty Will, we shall recover and also enjoy the blessings (spoils) beyond what we had before our calamity occurred. When this happens, give praise and glory to God and not to yourselves or your abilities. It is GOD Who brings us to recovery!

Breathtaking Moments

Someone has said that *"... life isn't measured by the number of breaths we take, but by the moments that take our breath away."* Such breathtaking moments often define our lives. There have been many such events in my fifty-nine years of life. Please allow me to share some of them with you.

In 1988, after driving cross-country from Georgia to Arizona, my wife, two children and I, stood for the first time on the precipice of the Grand Canyon and gazed in absolute awe at such a glorious wonder. It was an exciting moment which literally took my breath away for a few seconds. My children and I then took the Bright Angel Trail the following day, on foot, to the banks of the Colorado River; another special moment, indeed!

In 2008, I stood 16,000+ feet high in the Andes Mountains of Ecuador on the equator at 0 degrees latitude and longitude. I had only previously read about this place in history books.

In one of my mission trip ventures, I found myself in Guyana, South America, with a team of short-term missionaries. We took a trip up the Apure River in the Amazon basin to visit a couple of elderly missionaries who have spent many years there among the indigenous Indians who still live in thatched-roof huts and are barely dressed. As we made the long trip upriver in dug-out canoes, our Indian guides warned us not to put our hands in the river for it was full of piranha (flesh-eating fish)! Later that afternoon, we would fish with only a string and hook to catch our dinner for the evening. It was, as you may have already guessed Piranha! They were delicious.

At the top of the Eiffel Tower in Paris, France, I viewed that massive city in its grandeur. I've seen New York City from the top of the Empire State Building with my son, Jonathan, and would never take anything for that experience with my son. I've hiked over the White Cliffs of Dover near Brighton, England, all by myself. I've been inside an old German bunker on the French-German border, looked out to sea from a mountaintop in Barcelona, Spain; lived with natives in the Amazon region of South America. I've stood in front of Yosemite's huge monolith in California, and looked up at climbers on the face of El Capitan—amazing!

I've either led or have been a team-member on 68 foreign mission trips, well over 50 national trips for hurricane or tornado recovery, and have witnessed lives being changed by the almighty grace of God. But none of these compare to that awesome night in 1969, McRae, Georgia, when I turned my life over to Jesus Christ and accepted Him as my personal Lord and Savior. That was the moment which has defined my entire life and has enabled all of these experiences I have mentioned herein. I am convinced that without Christ in my life, none of these trips and events would have happened. That was truly the defining moment that took my breath away and replaced it with the Breath of God (The Holy Spirit)! To God be the glory for every blessing in my rich and wonderful life as a Christian believer.

Receiving a "Rhema" Word From God

The Bible utilizes words, phrases and sentences to impart God's message to His people. If we are to discern the will of God for our lives, we must be able to "hear" that word and know it as the voice of our Lord. Romans 10:17 states that, *"faith cometh by hearing, and hearing by the word of God."* The Greek understanding here for "word" is *Rhema*. Rhema is a word spoken to you at a particular time or moment in your life as encouragement or for instruction. It is specific in nature and not to be confused with another Greek word for "word" which is *Logos*. Logos is basically timeless in scope, whereas Rhema is time sensitive and for the moment.

The "Logos" (Word) of God, as we have it recorded in our Bibles, is ageless and timeless and reaches to all generations. Rhema is a refreshing word that comes to us in a moment; a word that is designed by God to touch and to heal; a word that is instant, even after one has patiently and faithfully awaited that word. It is God speaking through a friend, a particular passage of scripture, an experience through which we eventually hear that wee-small voice speaking to us. For Moses, it came through a burning bush in which the bush was not consumed. For both

Mary and Joseph, the Rhema came from an angelic proc-
lamation concerning their marriage to be and the ensuing
birth of our Savior, Jesus Christ.

Rhema may come to you at any time, any place,
through numerous means. It is God's refreshing Word for
a thirsty soul, a ray of light in the darkest nights of your
soul, a new hope in the midst of depression or defeat. It
may come suddenly and without notice, or even subtly
over an extended period of time. The key to "hearing" it
however, is to live by faith with expectation that God is
going to speak to *your* particular situation at *this* particular
time in your life.

Another Greek lesson may be in order here for us to
better understand our concept and God's concept of
"time." There are two important Greek words for time—
Chronos and *Kairos.* Chronos comes from the word
"chronological" which implies measured time (i.e. clocks,
calendars). Kairos is a serendipitous time, God's time,
which cannot be measured. It is in God's Kairos time that
He speaks this Rhema word to us as we faithfully await
His response.

In what appeared to be one of the darkest moments in
my life recently, I experienced several Rhema words from
God and was eventually lifted from my despair and de-

pression. God used some of my dearest friends to bring that Rhema word to me. One such friend, knowing my dilemma, dropped by and said that God had given him a specific word for me (Rhema)! "You're gonna make it. No matter how bad it may appear at the moment, you're gonna make it. Just keep on doing what you do best and know that God is going to bring ultimate victory!"

WOW! That was actually the Rhema I needed in my despairing moment. Others would then call, write, or pray for me and, in each instance, refreshed my soul.

There is that poignant and tender moment in II Corinthians 7:5-10, when the aged Apostle Paul remembers one true friend, Onesiphorous, who took him in and gave that great old Apostle food to eat and a place to stay. Paul speaks of him with awe and reverence when he declares, "He (Onesiphorous) often *refreshed* me with his visits; may the Lord have mercy on his household." One translation has it this way: "His visits to me were like a breath of fresh air. Many a time he braced me up."

I really like that story. It speaks volumes for those who have "braced me up" in life as dear friends and have ministered to me. I shall always be thankful to them for being open to the Rhema of God. My life has been surrounded with many like Onesiphorous, and have imparted to me a "breath of fresh air."

Are you dealing today with some heavy stuff in your own personal life? Are you going through one of those dark nights of the soul? If you are, then you certainly need a Rhema word from the Lord. Pray, read the scriptures, be still and await patiently that refreshing word. It may come from a friend, an acquaintance, a scripture. or our Lord's voice to you through the quietude of your spirit. Do not allow "self" or Satan to destroy that Rhema, but be ready to respond when you hear it. It will be refreshing to your weary soul.

May God bless you in these kairos moments of anticipation. I know some of you may be about ready to toss in the towel, but don't; God is not finished with you yet. Be faithful and patient and your refreshing will soon come.

A God-Shaped Hole
In My Heart

I remember gathering at our neighbor's home that day and watching the first moon walk back in the 1960s. Neil Armstrong's famous words still resound in my ears to this day as he made that first impression in the soil of the moon's surface: "That's one small step for man; one giant leap for mankind." I was only a young teen, but I remember vividly watching our neighbor's old black and white television screen as the snowy pictures were transmitted to earth from deep space. I remember thinking how amazing it was to send people into space and to actually land and walk on the surface of the moon. Our people wanted to know if there was any intelligent life out there and if the moon had any usable resources for use on earth. Experiments were to be done which would hopefully enable mankind to find new ways of doing things.

Can you begin to fathom the resources and knowledge it took to create a spacecraft capable of traveling such a distance from earth and then actually landing a lunar module with humans inside on the moon? It is simply mind-boggling to comprehend such a feat, yet there we were, watching it all unfold before our eyes! Amazing!

Humans have always sought answers from the universe. We've wanted to know more, spending billions of dollars in the process of gleaning such information. It's as though we have a God-shaped hole in our hearts that must eventually be filled in order for us to be whole and complete beings. Companies actually hire people to do nothing more than to serve them in a "Think Tank." A Think Tank looks ahead and plans for the future and seeks to resolve common issues for the benefit of a company.

Our lives are planned around calendars and clocks. We live by scheduled appointments because our lives have become so busy and complicated that we need something to follow and to keep us on track. We set the alarm clock to wake us on time. We set the coffee maker to have a fresh morning brew when awakening. We plan each hour of the day with our agendas and lose ourselves in following a scripted existence.

But there are those we usually envy who move to the beat of a different drummer; they expand the horizons we all live underneath; they explore the greatness of realms beyond where we dare not trod for fear of the unknown. We watch them in awe as they "go for the gusto." We applaud them following their accomplishments and wish we only had nerve enough or heart enough to follow. Yet, we remain firmly attached to earth and our present reality, never venturing further. We allow circumstances and situations to rule our world. We stick to the clock and calendar as they run our lives. In the back of our minds we think of what might have been had we the nerve or gumption to attempt the unknown, venture the high-road, hitch our dreams to a star. There will always be a God-shaped hole in our hearts. When we finally fill that void with the love, mercy and grace of such a caring God, our lives begin at that point to take on new meaning, new visions, and a new world before us.

It is my fervent prayer that you will discover that new life in Christ. Allow Him entrance into your hearts and He will fill the void.

On Earthquakes and God

Alejuela, Costa Rica—March 10, 1988

I felt the earth move tonight under my feet in Costa Rica. It literally shook the park bench I was sitting on with two other missionary friends. What an awesome experience! For the first time in my life, I felt the pent-up fury of the earth beneath us as it quivered and trembled, causing the pavement under our feet to slightly move up and down. The quake registered 5.6 on the Richter scale but registered an unforgettable reminder to me that there is more to this world than my small, often insignificant thoughts and existence. The earth moves with or without me. I have no control over it.

God was very real to me in those few brief moments in Costa Rica. I witnessed His awesome power and strength that is often beyond our comprehension. I knew, however, that He had everything in control. We all returned to our quarters for the night at the Methodist Center and I slept like a baby, knowing that my God was still on His throne.

The following day we received news that the earthquake had been 6.5 in the area further south where we had worked all week, and we wondered if any damage had been done to the small Methodist Church we had helped to construct. It would be a few years later, upon a return trip to the area, that I visited that church to discover that it had survived the quake with minor damage, while many of the other structures in the area had been destroyed!

Our God is an awesome and mighty God. His works are constantly on display, and His universe is constantly moving and changing. We are like small ants upon this round ball, owing our very existence to the Creator of it all—God. We must seek His presence in our lives if we are to be whole and complete. I challenge you today, if you have not yet met the Master, to do so by opening your hearts to receive Him as your personal Lord and Savior! God bless you, my friend.

Revival in Brighton, England

The gentle, verdant hills of England beckoned just beneath the circling Boeing 777 airliner as we made our approach for landing at Gatwick International Airport. Looking with eager eyes to catch a glimpse of London below, I viewed flats with rustic corrugated tile roofs, aligned in curved and straight little rows. Small streams of water came up from the English Channel and seemed to disappear into the lush, green hillsides. Sheep and cattle were grazing on many of those hills, while my heart leaped with the anticipation of discovering the world below.

This was dear old England—the land of Shakespeare and many other greats who had help shape and mold my life as it is today. From these very shores, worlds were launched and many were conquered. I was determined to see as much of her as I could during my brief stay of eight days. I would later realize that I could only scratch the surface of her vastness, for she was immense.

Methodists were everywhere—4,000 plus—catching every available bus or train to Brighton-by-the-Sea where the World Methodist Conference would convene. It was a bit overwhelming to be in the presence of so many Methodists in one place! They came here from India, Africa, Brazil, Venezuela, Panama, China, Taiwan, Milwaukee, New York—Georgia. Nearly every nation where Methodism exists was represented. Friendships were made which will last a lifetime. Great music, preaching, fellowship, and an overwhelming concern for the current state of our world brought us here to seek answers. We received them when commissioned to return home and continue to fight for freedom, justice and peace in our little corner of the world.

What a life and faith-transforming experience! I can truthfully say that the Methodist Church is still very much alive and well across the world and growing in massive numbers in foreign countries. We must all now catch the vision and share the dream and spirit of our founder—John Wesley.

In England, I felt my heart "strangely warmed."

Ben's Profound Statement

Many of you have heard me talk about my first grand-child, Benjamin and some of the quotes he has made in the first five years of his life. I guess it is the right and privilege of every grandparent to brag about their grand-children. Here's the latest from Ben and his most profound statement. Keep in mind that he has just entered Pre-K this year and has been spouting off wisdom with every breath.

Last Sunday, my wife and I were sitting with Ben at the dinner table when my wife, Renee, stressed to Ben that he should eat the beans on his plate because God would not be pleased with him if he did not. Ben looked at Grandma and asked if he could use her phone to call God and ask him about it. Renee told him that he couldn't reach God on her telephone. As quick as a wink, he responded by stating, "Then you need to get a better telephone!"

Out of the mouth of babes! What a response, and so simple. Why can't we communicate with God? WE CAN! If only we would spend quality time in prayer for He hears us when we pray. God is more than willing to hear us and to respond! Try Him today.

Prayers for Haiti

Years ago, I had the experience of going to Haiti while on a Volunteers in Mission work team. The atrocities I witnessed of how the people live were appalling. I could not believe my eyes, even after the sights I had seen on numerous occasions in other third-world countries. Poverty was rampant. People survived on so little, and their homes were cardboard shacks or shacks made from whatever they could glean from the dumps in the area. Stones held down the tin on most of the roofs, but the rains would still come through in places.

America is so blessed! We lived in the very lap of luxury. We are blessed with cars to drive, shopping centers where we can spend our money and every imaginable thing being offered to us at the lowest discount prices. And yet, we are most miserable! The people of Haiti are loving people who work wholeheartedly in a spirit of togetherness and concern for one another.

It breaks my heart when the television news shows the children running rampant and screaming in the streets following a recent earthquake there. Thousands are homeless now and are eating whatever they can find in the dumps.

Quickly, however, our U.S. has mobilized and has been sending help from various quarters. We have not turned a blind-eye to the plight of the situation, but have quickly immersed ourselves in their recovery through such wonderful efforts as the U.N., American Red Cross, Doctors Without Borders, and other mission agencies. Yet, there is still much work to be done. Restoration will depend upon you and me through our gifts of love, concern, prayer and charity.

There is an old saying, usually attributed to the Rev. John Bradford of the mid 1500s which states,

> *I too, like someone seen to have suffered mis-*
>
> *fortune, might have suffered a similar fate,*
>
> *but for God's mercy.*

Most of us would paraphrase that as saying, "There but for the grace of God go you and I."

Why not consider a monetary gift today to one of the organizations or many others who are still helping with the recovery efforts in Haiti? Be a blessing to others.

In Childhoods of the Mind

In verdant fields of childhood,
the landscapes of my mind
create a glow of yesteryears,
transcending space and time.
There, rugged, rough and ready,
made so by work and play,
I run those fields of clover
and dance all fears away.

I picked the fields of harvest,
loaded melons by the score;
Felt one with earth and nature,
and always yearned for more.
Then time became an enemy,
the years so quickly flew.
I sought to stop it constantly,
but nothing would subdue.

The transformation had begun
from boy to full-grown man.
I cannot slow the hands of time;
they move to purposed plan.
And here I sit in slumber ease
and dream of days gone by;
Still moving toward those hands of fate,
without whimper or a sigh!

Somewhere in precious memory,
the child within still roams
Those fields of verdant childhood,
and longs for hearth and home.
There is an emptiness within,
a void that's never filled;

When soon we leave our childhood,
 o'er Time's majestic hill.

But, oh, how sweet to dream about
 those graceful days of yore;
 When life, in all its fullness,
still yearned for something more!
Now, as you lay me down to rest
 beneath these hills of green,
Be well assured my soul has found
 its final rest—serene.

And do not weep for me, dear friend,
 but cry for all mankind
Who yearns for fields of verdant green
 in childhoods of the mind!

For Meghan

Will anyone notice
if I fail to show on Monday morning,
or never seek to run for President?
Will anyone care
if I miss the Bloodmobile
and fail to make this a better world?
Who should take notice
if I simply called it quits and
walked quietly away
without a thought or gesture
of remorse?
Will the stock market rise or decline
because of my passing?
Will the war in Iraq change at all
if I fail to buy war bonds?
Will anyone be concerned
if I do not show at the PTA tonight?
Will my departure be noticed
by anyone left behind?

The answer—a resounding YES!
As I grip the precious, tiny hands
of my new granddaughter
and know that one day
I will mean the world to her
as she does to me today!

For my Granddaughter—
Meghan Marie Monahan

Haircuts, Visions and
Perceptions

Some years ago I made a terrible "boo-boo" which actually turned into a blessing. I was trimming my beard with one of those electric razors and decided to thin the hair around my ears with it as well. In the process, I cut too deep and ran a streak through my hair that couldn't be repaired! My wife had to trim my entire head at that point to salvage my situation. I felt terrible! I had not had hair that short since the seventh grade of school!

The more I looked at myself in the mirror, the more I began to like the new look. It began to wear on me and people started telling me how much they liked the "new" me. So I began to develop an entirely new perception from the situation, and quickly turned that "boo-boo" into a blessing.

Perhaps we, too, need to learn how to look at each situation in our lives from a different perspective from time to time. Instead of the same mundane approaches to our every day events, perhaps we need to put ourselves in the other person's shoes and look at life a bit from his or her perspective. It could be a blessing in disguise.

Furthermore, I would seek to grow through a new outlook on life when those terrible moments come our way. Someone has said that a "Burden is a blessing in disguise." Why not unveil the flesh of the matter and see the blessing that may be awaiting you. Through such experiences we grow as individuals. Think positively and creatively. Delve within your inner soul and draw out the blessings awaiting you there. You'll be most glad you made the effort. Believe me, I KNOW!

Surgical Procedure

A writer,
with pen and ink,
sets forth his skill
to cut through skin and flesh
to the heart of the matter.
Deep, within the recesses of the darkest soul,
he extrudes the secrecies,
hidden thoughts
to reveal reality.
He sharpens the scalpel
and cuts right to the bone—
through the dead weight of matter,
and rests not his quill
until contentment is found.

With sure and steady hand
he draws forth upon the written line
all that embodies himself,
his inner soul, his heart;
leaving not a trace of scar-tissue
to gather and form.
Job now done,
he sits and grooms
as a fowl fresh from his prey
who has feasted upon the manna
and has been made full.

Yet, with urgency in his demeanor,
he rushes again into the surgical scar
to retrieve another thought,
another secret,
another passage . . .

Weary now from his task,
he sits back and awaits
the healing ointment of his soul
to mend the cut,
the tear,
to transform the patient
until the need again demands
his destined skill.

Code Blue!

Flashing lights and metal carts
are wheeled into the room;
Signals of a failing heart,
and one's impending doom.

Angels, white, rush to and fro,
Hectic pace to save;
Another victim slowly goes
beyond the bright light's haze.

My heart is fading very fast,
it signals my "Code Blue."
I pray for rescue now at last,
Could my angel of mercy be YOU?

O heart of my heart, my vital sign,
Take now my being and make it thine!

Beggars for Jesus

A few years back I was invited to do a Sunday evening youth event at one of our large area churches in Macon, Georgia. I carried my guitar and performed a mini-concert for the large group of youth. I truly enjoy sharing my faith with groups of teenagers and have done this for many years.

The youth minister, who introduced me to the group, surprised me by his witness while telling the assemblage about his first encounter with me nearly twenty years ago. It was in Waycross, Georgia, and I had been the youth week speaker for his church. I can barely remember the event now, but he will *never* forget it (as he implied) for it was during one of my concerts and ensuing testimony that this young man gave his life to Christ and began the journey of a lifetime!

The young man talked about how he had been lured to the event that night by some friends, and he had reluctantly gone. While there, the Holy Spirit moved upon his life and drew him in. He identified his broken life with things I had shared in my testimony. During the altar call I gave that night, he came forward and made his decision to live for Christ. From that point, he began to think and to act differently and to forge a new beginning. Today, he is a very happy and faithful disciple of Christ and continues to work with youth and the church on a full-time basis. How wonderful it is to know that my life touched another life twenty years ago and served to make such a tremendous impact! I was totally elated by his witness and could not help crying during his moving introduction.

He stated that following the concert he and his friends had planned to leave the church and go out and smoke some "pot" they had secured. That night's service changed that young man's life and direction forever!

We never know, do we, how many lives we touch along the journey of life! If we remain faithful and committed, following God's Will, He will produce the fruit from our labors. There will be even more fruit now and in the years to come because of my dear friend's witness. It's the "ripple-effect" that is created whenever we share our faith with others.

It has often been said that "evangelism is one beggar telling another beggar where to find bread." May we all be beggars for Jesus, showing others the way to eternal salvation and the goodness of God. Thanks, Clay, for making my life and ministry complete!

Miracle in Panama

Some years ago, I took a trip to Panama City, Panama, with *Volunteers in Mission*, under the great leadership of my dear friend, the Rev. George Herndon. This was a team of United Methodist short-term missionaries. Our goal was to repair a church and completely install new roof trusses and a roof near the Panama City airport. The church had recently been bombed, unintentionally, by American planes during the Manuel Noriega capture. Being near the airport, the small church received a considerable amount of damage. My particular job was to weld the trusses together at the apex.

It had been a very hot and humid week, and I had been sweating profusely while on top of the ladder which held me up to do my work. Two women held the base of the ladder while I worked above. I had just welded two joints together when the ladder began shaking. The wind was whipping across the airport area and became very blustery. I nearly lost my balance, but managed to reach back up to grab something in order to prevent me from falling. The only thing to grab happened to be the very hot trusses I had just welded together! My right hand was burned badly inside my palm. I quickly came down from

the ladder and our team medic put some antibiotic oint-
ment on the burn, wrapped it in a Vaseline gauze, and
gave me a pain pill. It was late afternoon and we had one
more day in which to complete the trusses and roof, but I
had three more trusses to weld before the team could put
the sheathing on. I was the *only* team member willing to
do that and who knew how to weld.

That night at camp, the entire team placed their hands
on me at the dinner table and prayed in earnest for God's
healing. Afterwards I went to bed and tried to sleep with
the pain, but could only doze in and out for brief periods
of time. Around 3 a..m., I got out of bed without disturb-
ing anyone and went outside where I sat down near a
street light. Suddenly realizing that the pain had subsided,
I decided to unwrap the gauze on my hand to see how
badly burned it was. What I witnessed was nothing short
of a miracle! My hand showed NO scar or sign of having
been burned at all! It was completely healed!

Quickly I ran back inside and awakened everyone
with the exciting news. We all began to celebrate the
mighty healing power of God! Needless to say, we were
able to finish the church that day and put the roof on. We
held a service that night for all the folks in the community

and related the story to them. Everyone began celebrating and excitedly coming to the altar for prayer and praise!

Needless to say, our team members will never forget the amazing power of such a great and mighty God who is STILL in the miracle working business. Trust in Him today and be filled with His grace and mercy.

"Legal" Aliens

My wife hit a deer on her way to work the other morning causing $3,200 worth of damage. It was still dark when she caught a glimpse of the big buck out of the corner of her eye (she saw his "rack" of horns). We've had a rental car for two weeks now and, even with good car insurance, we have to pay 20% for the rental as well as a $200 deductible on car repairs! Consider this as a very expensive hunting trip in order to "bag a buck!"

Renee, my wife, could have easily lost her life that morning, and we are both keenly aware of that. The expense could have been enormous to my family and me, as it has been for thousands of families nationwide who have lost loved ones over such a tragic end.

I remember vividly when the first deer were transplanted from the North down to the piney thickets of south Georgia. It was back in the early 1950s and I recall how folks would go out to Little Ocmulgee State Park near McRae, Georgia (my hometown), and sit in their cars at lakeside to watch the deer come out of the woods to drink from the lake. As they so quickly multiplied, the state of Georgia soon instituted hunting days for deer. It has now become a major industry in the state, and if you consider the costs involved in each wreck that occurs because of them, it becomes a huge monetary burden on society, especially for those who could care less about a hunting season for deer! Deer could never replace the many lives lost.

Many of us complain about the "illegal aliens" who cross our borders from Mexico and come to our country to take our jobs and place huge burdens on our state in order to help our farmers and corporations. In similar fashion, I consider deer as our "legal aliens," who were brought here for hunters and their industry. Our woods and backyards are now full of these pesky critters in alarming numbers. As our number of "illegal aliens" grow, so, too, does the number of "legal aliens."

Our states spend millions of dollars annually to make our roadways safe for motorists, but how much are they spending to keep motorists safe from our "legal aliens?"

I realize I'm on my soapbox here, but I feel that we need to do something about this dilemma before any more lives are taken and millions are spent on car repairs or replacements. My wife has a co-teacher at her school who has already been hit by deer three times this year while on her way to work; once while in her rental car!

I have nothing against hunters, but let's get real here. There are dangerous aliens around us every time we set out on the highways, thus posing a real threat to our health and well-being. Insurance rates continue to escalate due to the number of accidents, claims and deaths related to deer. What can ultimately be done about this major problem? If left unattended, it will only escalate. Next time, God forbid, it could be you or one of your loved ones. Should you wait until that happens, or will you also become an advocate against this growing danger? I'll leave the solution up to you and your actions. Be careful out there!

In Prayer

(Published first in "The Reach of Song," 1996-1997
by The Georgia State Poetry Society, Inc.)

In all my search for understanding,
Vain attempts to find my way—
This world had none to offer,
Though I searched both night and day.

Through endless days and empty nights,
I looked most everywhere;
Still the answers would not come
Until I bowed in prayer.

I found peace and great contentment,
And the longings of my soul;
When I surrendered to my Father,
Then the Master made me whole.

For He knew my every weakness,
And my search for love and care.
I've never stood so tall in life
As when I knelt that day in prayer!

Was Jesus a Liberal!

By all definitions, Jesus would have been a liberal. He would not have fit into our neat little political parties of today. He was friend to the downtrodden, the blind, lepers, the deaf and dumb, prostitutes and others on the fringes of society. His worst enemies were those of the temple—the Sanhedrin, the Pharisees and Sadducees. They were always in conflict over his actions and philosophies, and eventually concocted a clever scheme to have him arrested and crucified. His message was TOO liberal: *"Love one another"* - *"Forgive one another."* It was to the rich young ruler that Jesus said for him to go and sell whatever he had and to give it to the poor. He blessed the broken and lashed out at the money changers in the temple. He was more concerned with ONE lost soul than many righteous ones.

Jesus cannot be boxed into a neat little package to fit your agendas for when you think you have him figured out, he totally surprises you with a change in direction. Without being disguised, he was a master of disguises. He literally confuses the person seeking to make sense of him.

Thus, the Savior of the world becomes a paradox for us with a new and controversial paradigm. We want him on "our" side, but he doesn't quite fit. He's never a right-extremist, or left, and that bothers us. Why couldn't he just say that he was Democratic or Republican and be done with it? We could then choose sides and be done with the issue. And yet, Jesus embodies the very best of both parties—the good we all represent.

Even when those who loved Jesus attempted to show their loyalty, He would always counter. His disciples never knew exactly how to respond to Him. They were always confused but knew (beyond the shadow of a doubt) that he was REAL and a REALIST. He was always there for the disciples whenever the going got tough. He'll also be there for you whenever you call upon His precious Name.

Lift high the banner of Christ today and find new life in His love, mercy and grace. To God be the glory!

Pot-Liquor Hill

Seems like an eternity has passed, yet I still recall vividly that special little place of my youth—Pot-Liquor Hill. It's actually the place of my childhood, those awkward formative years when I learned most of the important lessons that would serve to carry me through.

In the 1950s, Pot-Liquor Hill was a simple little ridge just outside of Helena, Georgia. It was a small community above the railroad tracks which flourished with small farms and beautiful flower gardens. Families depended on each other and were always neighborly. Most people walked back then because cars were a luxury for those who could afford them. I remember only one family on the Hill owning a TV (black and white set), and we all gathered at that house on the day that John F. Kennedy was buried. Dad finally bought us a black and white TV when I was around twelve, and we watched the first man walk on the moon, which my father (God rest his soul) never believed happened. He considered it a hoax by our government to prove to the Russians that we had the ability to do such a thing!

I remember *Gunsmoke, Rin-Tin-Tin, Leave It To Beaver, The Lone Ranger* and other great shows of my childhood. Those shows always had a good guy fighting against evil. The guy in white always won. I remember getting a set of the Lone Ranger's guns one Christmas and that was the highlight of my life at that point. For a couple of years I saved the folks on Pot-Liquor Hill from all the bad guys, defending them with my two plastic pistols with the little round white bullets! Even though my guns were fake, I really believed I was doing justice.

"Pot Liquor" is the juice that develops when turnip greens are cooked. We used to crumble cornbread into that juice in a bowl for a really tasty meal. But we also had other "liquors" on the Hill that were created using corn-mash and certain other lethal ingredients. Those pint bottles of "shine" were sold in various locations. People who knew where the stills were located never breathed a word about them to the law for fear that someone in their own family could have been involved.

Giles' Grocery Store was across the tracks at the bottom of the Hill. It was my favorite place to go, for there I could see all of the latest products on the market. I remember taking a quarter and buying an ice-cold R.C. Cola, a chocolate Moon-pie, and a few Red Hots. I would still having some change left over! We bought our kerosene for starting fires in our pot-bellied stove from Giles'. Kerosene was cheaper than wood, plus it was easier to be had in those days. Finding and cutting wood was an arduous task, so we mostly burned kerosene.

Life on the Hill evolved around the Turpentine Still. Trucks lined up at the Still most days to deliver their barrels of pine tar for processing into resin. The tar had to be cooked in huge tanks and brought to a boil and then skimmings were drawn-off and placed in metal barrels where the resin would then harden. The rest of the mix would flow down a small creek near our house to a couple of holding ponds in the nearby woods. You could literally see the steam on the stream of water as it flowed from the still to the woods. Many of the men on the Hill earned their living working at the Still or for the woodsmen who harvested the tar. (*The E.P.A. would have a field-day with a company like the Still today! It would be ruled unsafe, without a doubt.*)

Boys on the Hill would get picked up every morning during the summer to work on truck farms where we could earn as much as $5.00 for a full day of work. We used to load crops of various kinds and truck them into McRae to sell. The days of work were very long, hot, and usually lasted from before sunlight to well after dark. I remember many times going to my cousin's chicken barns and catching chickens at night for $5.00. Chickens can't see you at night, so we would go into the barns and catch the hens and put them into wooden crates, and the older boys would load them onto flatbed trailers. It was indeed a very hard job that yielded many cuts and gashes on your hands from the claws of the chickens.

We always gave momma some of our money to help with groceries. We were always short on funds and had to rely heavily on our family garden. Pickling and putting up fruits and vegetables was a common summertime activity around the Cravey house, and everyone knew the importance of it for the coming winter months. It helped us through those winters until the crops came in again.

Back then we lived by the rule that "if you don't work—you don't eat!" And so we all grew up with a strong work ethic firmly implanted. We knew what we had to do, and so we did it, although sometimes reluctantly. It was hard work.

The Hill had its share of calamities but families would always come to your aide whenever needed. If a family had someone sick, we would all throw in some vegetables, canned goods, food stock, or other items to help that family get back on their feet again. This was the local "Welfare" department back then where people really took care of each other. Today, everyone wants a government hand-out! Funny how times have changed.

I experienced my first girlfriend on Pot-Liquor Hill, played my first game of baseball there, played hookey more than once while in elementary school, got more spankings there than I care to recall, and fell in love with life (as we knew it) in that special place of my memory. It will always be a part of me, even though things have changed there a good bit. The Still closed many years ago and is now grown-up in weeds, merely a semblance of what once existed. And I guess that I am as well, only a semblance of those good-ole days on Pot-Liquor Hill and my childhood.

The Rhythm of Life

Layers of dark clouds began floating in across the barren, crisp and wintry sky. CNN has reported a potential nor-easter for the area later today. I sit in contemplation, observing an act of nature developing without my help, without so much as a whimper, moan or sigh. Through the leafless trees of my back yard, my eyes are drawn to squirrels busily scampering about, searching for nuts to prepare for the long, cold days ahead. Overhead, a beautiful flock of Canadian Geese fly in broken formation as they stride in rhythmic motion across the endless sky towards the horizon and beyond.

With a loud rumble and screeching stop, the city's trash men pull to the curb out front and busy themselves with emptying a week's supply of trash into their already full cache, then quickly they jump back onto the sides of the truck and move forward to the next stop. In rhythm, perhaps without much notice, these men carry out their daily purpose, carrying away the residue and discarded elements of our lives.

The alarm goes off on the nightstand right on time, and I rise from my morning cup of Columbian Supreme then walk to the bedroom to shut off the clamor. The clock has been my daily reminder, faithfully waking me for years without failure. It is a welcoming, yet alarming sound. Its rhythm is steady and sure. That's the way I like things in my life.

I jump hurriedly into the shower to begin the rituals of my hectic day. My thoughts turn suddenly to the history test I'll sit and take in a couple of hours. It is my final college exam, and I'm anxious to get it over with in order to graduate next week.

Late December. Christmas break begins tomorrow and graduation will be held next Saturday morning. My mind is filled with preparations, invitations and such. What's next for me? Where will I go and what will I do with the rest of my life? Would that my life had the same purposed rhythm as nature, and yet, it does! Decisions have to be made, many of which will determine the entire course of my life.

There is a rhythm to everything, even this shell of a man, this contradiction in terms. With pen in hand, I move towards the greatest test of all—LIFE!

Coming Home
(An Essay)

Golden crested trees lined the small lane through the woods which led to the old home place. There, at the far end, stood an old rustic log cabin, hand-hewn from virgin pine generations ago. The old house sagged in the middle due to the supports underneath giving way from age. It was in bad repair, much like my own spirit. I came here perhaps seeking a miracle, perhaps just solace, perhaps a respite from the busyness of my life, hopefully to draw from the voices of my past. Would they speak once again and give renewal to this weary pilgrim? I had to know, for my life had reached the turning point, a crossroad, a time of decision. Mid-life does that to us, I am told. We try to get in touch with those things of the past which helped us make sense of it all and once gave structure and meaning to our lives.

I sat on the hood of my car in front of the cabin and just stared at it, reminiscing. I remembered some ghosts of the past. It was there, on that long stretched of porch, that my father used to sit with me and talk about life.

"Always remember, Son," he would say, "always remember who you are and where you came from. Never take anything for granted. Always be able to look at yourself each day in the mirror and be proud of who you are. Go slowly, and at an unhurried pace along the way. Remember to always make time for the things which are most important in your life, and remember that life is very fleeting; don't put off things that you should take care of NOW.

His words came back as clear to me as a ringing bell . I could see his weathered old face, wrinkled by the years from pain and crop failure. I could sense again his strength as a "survivor" who had fought well his countless battles and had lost a few and won a few. I had learned a wealth of knowledge on that old front porch, and dad had been my teacher, my mentor.

It was from that porch I first launched into the new world—beyond the woods—beyond the little lane—beyond my comfortable surroundings—the day I first stepped onto that old yellow school bus which would take me to school and beyond. There I learned of other worlds and other people, cultures, places I had only heard of. I learned how to communicate, to decipher, to play base-ball, football, and basketball. I met some friends in first grade who have been friends for life. There, I learned how to love, to lose, and the pain that comes from both. My horizons expanded far beyond that place of childhood to a brave new world alive with possibility and adventure. And yet, those words once spoken by my father have sustained me through these years and have given me strength and consolation to this day.

Listen! I could almost hear my father's voice as I sat on the hood of my car and remembered the past. Today, I came home again.

Music As A Religion

The first words I recall were from a lullaby my mother used to sing beside my bed. In her calm and tender alto voice, mama would soothe me off to sleep and into dreamland. Music has always been an integral part of my life. Every song on the radio serves as a reminder of some thing or some one in my past.

Otis Redding's song, "Sitting on the Dock of the Bay" played for the first time on WDAX radio in McRae, Georgia, on a hot July afternoon when I was fifteen. The disc jockey told us that Otis had just been killed in an air-plane crash and this was his last release. That very day was filled with thoughts of where I was going—what I planned to do with my life. It was made even more deci-sive by the singing of that black man from Macon, Geor-gia.

Pictures are vividly painted for me by the songs I hear. Those days in the 1960s, riding shotgun with my old friend, Thomas, listening to the radio and playing "Name That Tune," filled those long, hot, humid days of summer. Saturated now in my memory, they serve up a potpourri of thoughts: first date—first kiss—

I'll always be addicted to music. I'm that fellow who

wants all conversation to stop as soon as one of those smooth, mellow folk ballads comes on the radio. It's almost as if I'm bowing down before God Himself, by honoring the songwriter and the singer. I guess you could say that music is somewhat of a religion to me. I love it, respect it, sing it, play it! It demands an audience and my devotion.

From the lullabies my mother used to sing to the Wedding March I heard on my wedding day, to the song "Sweet Hour of Prayer" which was sung at my father's funeral—music has been an integral part of my life. When I pass, I can only hope that my family will honor me with lots of beautiful music at my funeral. Let it be a celebration, a sermon, a message of life that again accompanies me down the corridors of time and eternity!

Conditioned By Our
Surroundings

When I was ten years old, I remember so well the day
the circus came to town. The train arrived in McRae with
several box cars loaded with animals for the circus acts. It
was a Tuesday, and there would be a parade of the ani-
mals from the railroad station in McRae up to the fair-
grounds in Helena (approximately 1½ miles distance). I
played hookey from school that day with two of my bud-
dies, and we went to watch the parade. I will never forget
watching those giants of the runway parade up the high-
way. Included were big bull elephants, tigers, lions, gi-
raffes and zebras. I had never seen any of these animals
before, and it was a great thrill for me and my friends.

The men led those animals out of the box cars and
into the streets, and then began lining them up for the af-
ternoon parade through town. Once there, the circus peo-
ple would set up their three tents for the shows that night.

Once the circus crew and animals reached their desti-
nation, I was just standing around in awe of everything,
when the man in charge of the bull elephants asked me if I
wanted to help him set up his area. He offered me two free
tickets to the show that night, so how could I refuse?

That day I learned an important lesson on life and living. I was given the job of helping another man set-up the feed and water containers for the elephants. While doing this, I noticed that the largest bull elephant in the group was tied to a small, wooden stake by an attached sisal-rope. The stake was loosely driven into the ground. I was amazed and confused at the same time, so I began to query the circus worker as to why such a huge and danger-ous creature as the bull elephant didn't just pull up that small stake and go rampaging off through town. He then related the following story to me.

According to the caretaker of the elephants, the big bull was raised from a baby at their circus farm in Florida. While very young, the elephant was staked each day to a metal chain attached to an iron rod cemented into the ground several feet deep. Try as it would, the baby ele-phant could never pull up the stake from the ground. After weeks of attempts, in complete desperation, the baby ele-phant gave up its quest to be free of its chain and stake. The elephant, according to the circus man, had become "conditioned" to its surroundings and had accepted the fact that it would never be free from its captor.

The worker continued to share with me that now, many years later, the elephant had become so conditioned that they never had to worry about it wandering off. He said that the elephant had become just a docile little baby!

How quickly you and I become conditioned by the world around us. We allow it to dictate to us what we can and cannot do. From childhood, we discover what will and will not work, and never once do we venture beyond those boundaries. If we do, we are immediately met with ridicule and labeled by our societal standards as "weird," "strange," or "different."

There is that beautiful story in the first book of the Bible, Genesis, in which Abraham, God's faithful servant, is told (at the age of 75) to move to Haran, a far-off country. Abraham knows absolutely no one in Haran, but faithfully follows God's command to GO. He packs his family and livestock and moves out for this new land that God would provide. In doing so, Abraham became a blessing to many, and his story continues to inspire us today to move beyond the boundaries of our own little insecurities, our multitudinous problems, our very existence—to a world that awaits us with a blessing.

On the Meaning of Life

Strive for happiness, friend.
There is little comfort in great riches—
For they are as fleeting as time itself.
The ladder of success can never compare
To the richness of friends made,
Love received,
Shared lives.
One finds life through giving,
And not in taking.

Be a giver of all the graces given to you,
And truly you shall be
The richest of all mankind.
The grace supplied to you shall be
Your comfort and strength—
Your lighthouse in the darkest night;
A friend when others have failed you.

Strive for that which is
Far greater than life itself and
You shall find the true meaning of peace.
In an humble, contrite, and serving spirit,
You shall find life and the
Deeper meaning of eternity.

Our mortal lives are as but
Grains of sand along the shore,
Washing to-and-fro with every wave,
Being deposited,
Uplifted,
Moved again until, finally,
Being broken into millions of atoms and

Becoming part and parcel
Of the whole of life.

We must continue
Day after day,
Year after year,
Striving for the best in happiness,
Through grace,
In love,
For peace,
Filled with hope
and friendship.

Therein lies the hope of eternity
And the very face of God!

Harp-Strings of the Heart

Plucked for resonance,
Sound extruded,
Melodious tunes in part.
Soft vibrations,
Gentle persuasions,
Harp-strings of the heart.

You pulled and tugged,
Gave hope unto
These cold, hard strings of mine;
Brought endless joy,
The Craftsman's ploy,
Sweet melodies in time.

In dark depression,
My own recession,
I had all but given up;
Yet, soon I heard
Harp-strings and words
That filled my barren cup!

In contemplation,
Situations
Sought to rule my day;
Endless quests,
And little rest,
Drove my heart astray.

But softly still,
Against my will,
You plucked your melody;

Convincing darts
Thrown at my heart,
You set this captive free!

With gentle care,
You worked your ware,
And soon my heart gave way;
Received the gift,
Sweet spirits lift
My soul unto thy way!

Play ever on
Thy rapturous song,
Imploring unto me—
That life is for living,
'Tis far better giving
Your life as a symphony!

Each string of the heart,
A most vital part,
Played out in rhythm and rhyme;
Seeking its place,
In the human race—
A prodigal in its own time . . .

Cries out to be heard,
Through each note and word,
Expressed upon the harp-strings
of the heart!

Lament on Richard Cory

*(With apologies to Edwin Arlington Robinson's
"Ode to Richard Cory" - 1869-1935)*

He had it all together—
This Richard Cory man.
With grace he wooed the crowds that he passed by.
Silken threads from head to toe,
and gold upon his hands;
We stared at him and asked the question, "Why?"

Why should one so lucky
be singled out by all?
And why, pray tell, does he deserve the best?
We sat him on a pedestal
and leaned against the wall;
By him, we seemed to judge most all the rest.

But was he really lucky
to be born with silver spoons
Which fed him from the finest tableware?
Or was it a curse
to be blessed so soon,
And never to have earthly cares?

Oh, cursed life of struggle
That we must live each day!
Yet, sane, we move against the pain,
And pray for better days!

Just Reward

Just reward for job well-done,
You took the trophy in hand;
And gave your soul to the teeming crowds,
To that chattering bandstand.

Off you went upon your way,
Through passages of time;
Content to know that all your life
You'd live one purpose in mind.

To that very end for which you came,
An example of all we are—
You hung your love upon a cross,
And your kingdom to a star!

Your job now done in evening sun,
Trophy received as planned;
How could you have known your just reward
Would be nails driven through each hand?

An Unselfish Act

The televised commercial showed two sisters coming home from school, one a few years older than the other. The older sister opens a bag of cookies to discover that there is only one cookie left. Both children then stare at that one cookie until the older sister resolves the issue by reaching for the single cookie and handing it to her little sister—truly an unselfish act.

An act of TV magic then occurs as if God had ordained it from the beginning. When the older sister looks back at the cookie bag, a new cookie appears, exactly where the other one had been! What a wonderful ending to such a cute commercial. God provided for both due to the older sister's unselfishness.

Our unselfishness and caring attitudes toward others actually allows God the ability to work in very mysterious ways, often to the benefit of all concerned.

Thoughtful Friends

My dear friends, Hugh and Emelyn Hunter, just returned from their annual vacation. This year they visited Kauai, Hawaii, and had the time of their lives. While there, they purchased several bags of Kauai coffee for family and friends. Hugh was thoughtful enough to bring me a bag, which I have thoroughly enjoyed. Each time I make a brew of that rich, aromatic coffee, I am reminded of my dear friends and others like them who help me make it through each day.

As former members of my Sylvania church, Hugh and Emelyn are the "salt" of the earth to me. Hugh recently told me that he was still one of my biggest cheerleaders and appreciated my preaching style and personality. Such a statement as that means the world to me.

My heart is greatly saddened when I think of so many people who seem to be friend-less, some by their own choosing. I read somewhere that in order to have a friend, you must first *become* a friend. So true.

My dear friend, Gloria Pate, from Fort Gaines, Georgia, just called a couple of hours ago to see how I was doing. She wasn't concerned with herself, but with me! Her thoughtfulness is immeasurable and much appreciated in this crazy, hectic-paced world.

Dear old friend, Rev. Jack Taylor, also called a few minutes ago to lift me up. It seems he always knows exactly when to call. For some reason, God had just impressed upon him to call and ask how I was. Jack and I were roommates at Emory University years ago, and shared a lot in common. I would walk through fire for my dear, dear friend in Christ.

Yesterday, my trusted friend, Victor Wolfe, called just in time to brighten up my day. The day had gotten off to a dismal start, but Victor has the type of personality that could bring a bear out of winter hibernation! Thanks Victor for all you have done for me. May God grant an increase in your love and concern for others.

I could go on and on about the countless others who make my day and lift my spirits, but this book could not contain all of them. Suffice it to say that we all need friends, true friends, those who will be there through "thick and thin." May your numbers increase!

Living on High Cholesterol

I've just finished writing a new country song that carries the title of this article. It was created from many conversations I've had recently with friends who have been retired a few years now . Seems that once they retired, everything started falling apart, physically and mentally. The doctor's appointment becomes the highlight of their week. Another pill, another test, another bout with insurance . . . The list goes on and on. Makes me almost want to never retire!

Here's the chorus I wrote for that song:

I'm living on high cholesterol, drinking bottles of Geritol;
Buying everything on Social Security.
I've had every surgery known to man, and now I'm living
on the government plan.
This life I'm living will be the death of me!

Whatever happened to going to Hawaii, seeing the world, having the time of your life? Retirement for some is a nightmare. Also seems like those friends you once counted on to be there for you are always out of the loop when you need them now. It becomes a very lonely existence for many, but that could easily be resolved by keeping in the loop, getting active in different causes or organizations of older adults. Join a club; fight a cause.

Keep your mind sharp by reading as much as possible and never becoming addicted to that TV set. Take a kid fishing. Mentor a young person. Sign up for short-term mission trips where you could do a world of good for people in other countries. Life doesn't have to end here with all of your aches and woes. Step out in faith to accomplish something new. I have a friend who recently completed a course in technical college at 78 years young!

My dear friend, Rev. Henry Erwin of Waynesboro, Georgia, completely amazes me. He is 92 years old and is still an avid fisherman, woodworker, canoeist and great father and grandfather. His beautiful wife, Lila, passed about two years ago, but that did not slow Henry down. Henry's passion for life is summed up in a statement he shared with me a couple of weeks ago when I visited with him: "Charles, I don't have time to think about all of my problems. I've just got so much to do and things that I want to accomplish before I meet my Maker."

That's Henry for you. Always busy, anticipating his next work project, looking forward to each new day with anticipation and joy in his heart.

May we all get out of our doldrums and find that special place or project where we belong. Find joy again in your life by giving joy to others!

Life's Recipe

1 cup of good thoughts
1 cup of kind deeds
1 cup of consideration for others
2 cups of sacrifice for others
3 cups of forgiveness
2 cups of well-beaten faults

Mix these thoroughly and add tears of joy and sorrow and sympathy for others. Fold in 4 cups of prayer and faith to lighten other ingredients and to raise the texture to great heights of Christian living. After pouring all of this into your daily life, bake well with the heat of human kindness. Serve with a smile and God will bless and keep you in His great and abundant love!

Out of the Mouth of Babes

When our daughter Angie was five years old, she was out under the carport at play one day with a coffee can full of pennies and her mother's wooden ladle. She was stirring the pennies in the can with the ladle when I happened upon her. We had just returned home from morning worship at church where we had made a love-offering plea for some indigent people in our community. We then received an offering for the couple who were down on their luck.

When I questioned Angie as to what she was doing, her reply was very heart warming. She smiled and said, "I'm making more money for God to use to help others!"

Isn't that beautiful, coming from such a young child? Would that you and I could forget our own selfish motives and quests for living and getting ahead, and concentrate more upon what we can accomplish and do for God! If we would devote ourselves more to Him, He would take care of all our needs. He has already promised this in His Word.

When we think of God and put Him first in all things, He, in return, will bless and supply our needs. Devote more of your time, energies and efforts to Him today.

Moral and Spiritual Fog

Many people today seem to be wandering about in a sort of moral and spiritual "fog." They may actually be professing Christians, loving mothers and fathers, and may even be responsible citizens, but they have a tremendous feeling of helplessness in the face of the shifting values of our affluent and rapidly changing culture.

Jesus understood such feelings of lostness. In the fifteenth chapter of Saint Luke's gospel, we find three of Jesus' parables about a LOST SHEEP, a LOST COIN, and a LOST BOY. Jesus indicated in these parables that our lostness is of grave concern to the One who created us, and that there is a way by which the lost may be found. Let's consider for a moment our own feelings of lostness and ask three basic questions: 1) How did we get into this predicament? 2) Does anybody really care? 3) Is there an answer for us?

I believe our feelings of lost-ness can be linked directly to our "declining faith." We have simply lost faith in people. So whom do we look to? Our heroes have seemingly gone. We must turn therefore to Jesus and trust and believe fully in Him.

The great tragedy of our lives is that along with our

declining faith in people, there has been a corresponding decline in our faith in God. Many of us actually prefer our lost-ness. God forbid! Turn back to God, for He cares about your situation and your lost-ness and will enable you to return through that fog of moral and spiritual decay.

Is there a way out of this fog? Is there a cure for our lost-ness? Yes, indeed. There really is a loving God who cares deeply about you as an individual. It really does matter to Him what you do with your life. You can trust those values you were taught as a little child, and allow Christ to bring you back again from this depressing fog.

I trust that you will not fall prey to the overwhelming decline in faithlessness today, and instead, will return to the God of our fathers who seeks to bring us to a more holy and complete existence. Trust in Him today.

When My Mother
Used to Pray

The roads of life are narrow,
they seem to wind forever;
And men have often tried to go alone.
But the dangers and the trials,
the heartaches and the sorrows
Are much too hard for us to bear alone.

And so we seem to follow
some preordained direction;
looking for the strength to guide our way.
But for me my mind goes wandering
back to home and mama,
and the strength I'd find when mother used to pray.

She'd pray for better mornings,
and rain-clouds without warning.
She'd ask the Lord to help her children
all along life's way.
And she'd never forget His blessings,
and all the times He'd helped her.
Oh, I remember when mother used to pray!

I can still see mama sitting there
in her old gray-flannel gown,
Mending clothes and shelling peas
after we had gone to bed.
Her days were long and tiresome,
but she never once complained.
She never had much in her life
'cause she gave it to us instead!

Her faith was always strongest
when the storms of life would come.
She'd hold us close and pray those storms away.
Her faith now dwells within my blood,
And her life runs through my veins.
Oh, I remember when my mother used to pray!

*(Written for my dear mother, Mrs. Irene Cooper Cravey,
1922-2008, who gave me physical life and brought me to
the place where I could choose for myself the way that I
should go. I'll always be thankful to her for those early,
formative years, and those constant prayers for her chil-
dren's safety and well-being. God bless you, mama. I'll
always love you.)*

Mama Said Goodbye

I held her hand the very last time
while she lay on her nursing home bed.
As I started to leave, she looked up at me,
And with her eyes she tenderly said . . .

"My baby boy, I wish you well,"
Her staring eyes did say.
"Take good care and we'll meet again
On Heaven's shore one day."

And with those tender fleeting moments,
Watching Mama slowly die,
I felt those tears within me swelling
When Mama said goodbye!

Open My Eyes

Some years ago, the *Los Angeles Times* carried the poignant story of Anna Mae Pennica. She was blind from birth due to congenital cataracts. She had always thought that nothing could be done for her, but Dr. Thomas Pettit removed the cataracts one day and her corrected vision is now 20/30. She now eagerly looks forward to waking up every morning to see her beautiful new world. Dr. Pettit stated that there were surgical techniques available as far back as the 1940s that could have corrected her problem!

Think about it: for 40 years Anna Mae walked in darkness needlessly. If only someone with the knowledge of that surgical procedure could have shared it with Anna Mae, her life would have been totally different.

Perhaps someone today is awaiting your testimony and witness to the love, mercy and grace of Jesus Christ but you are withholding the Good News from them. We must be faithful and share God's goodness with others so they, also, may see!

Perhaps we ought to sing with more urgency that lovely old song . . . *"Open my Eyes that I may see, Glimpses of truth thou hast for me!"*

Seven Steps to a New Life

Let me share with you seven important steps on how you can have a brand new life, beginning today. I will introduce issues here that we all must face and decide upon daily.

1. **Decide where you want to go and what you want to do.** It is time that we stop meandering between where we are and where we would like to be. Do something about it. Change course, direction, catch a new vision of where you want to be in life and how you'll need to proceed in order to get there.

    "A journey of a thousand miles begins with a single step."

    Lao-tzu, *The Way of Lao-tzu*
    Chinese philosopher (604 BC - 531 BC)

2. **Pick your place.** Find out what it is that you do best. Those talents didn't just happen to you by chance. Then do the best you possibly can. You see, if you aim at nothing—YOU'RE SURE TO HIT IT!

3. **Be honest about your abilities.** If you're missing an

arm, you probably will not want to sign up for the high-bar in gymnastics! Take your most simple abilities and expand upon them in order to accomplish what you are capable of, one step at a time.

4. **Lay your past failures aside.** I know a lot of people who are unwilling to give up on their past failures and move forward to a new life. They are living lives of pity and disappointment. Have you ever seen a heart of disappointment accomplish anything? The Apostle Paul said, " . . . *forgetting those things which are behind, I press toward the mark"* (Philippians 3:13). Thoughts of past failures will crop up every now and then, but you just keep on walking, and the further you walk, the further behind they will be.

5. **Begin right where you are.** You want to preach? Well, try teaching a Sunday School class, or taking a youth group under your wings first, or being regular and faithful in your church. Get in there and attend Sunday morning, Sunday night worship services; attend Wednesday evening bible studies. Pay your tithes like you should, and perhaps start a home bible fellowship. If you want to be a secretary, then take typing

lessons or business classes. If you want to be a mechanic and live for God in doing that, start by doing oil changes and tune-ups—learn how to do those before you take your neighbor's Mercedes apart!

6. **Begin with what you have.** You see, ministry is as close as your own two hands. Jesus said that it's as simple as a cup of water given in His Name. You have two hands, which means you already have TWO ministries! That means that you've got more to do for mankind and for God than you'll ever get done in your lifetime—SO GET STARTED!

I remember a little poem from my childhood that goes like this:

"Shamgar had an ox-cart; Moses had a rod.
David had a slingshot, and all were used for God!"

7. **Do what you can do until you can do what you want to do.** I want to go over that once again because so many people tend to wait until they can do everything and because they can't do everything, THEY DO NOTHING AT ALL! So, here's where you

start—Do what you CAN do until you can do WHAT you want to. It's as simple as that. You will never be perfect although you should always strive towards perfection in life; do the very best you can with your limited resources.

Some of you have been to Florida and to Disneyworld and the Epcot Center. Some of you may have even been out to California to Disneyland. I want you to remember that it all started with a guy by the name of Walt Disney. Walt Disney was a meager, struggling little cartoonist who started out with just a MOUSE. Not just any mouse, however, but a PAPER MOUSE he had dreamed up out of his own brain.

John D. Rockefeller, Sr., was pushing a cart in New York City making 90 cents a day in his early years. And Jesus began as a babe in a hay manger without even so much as a place to lay His head. So whatever you are doing, friend—DON'T YOU DARE QUIT! HOLD ON! HOLD ON!

According to the Bible, God made man and woman out of DUST! So to get started in your new life and your new career, you don't have to have a lot of STUFF—take what you've got and use it for God and He will bless!

Life's Tempestuous Seas

Over life's tempestuous seas I've come,
and through the darkest night;
Yet, I have never traveled blind
for Jesus gave me sight.

And when those waves would o'er me roll,
His saving hands I knew
Would comfort, calm the raging seas,
and bring me safely through.

Whenever life's unending pain
prevails upon my soul,
I'll never fear, my Lord is near
to keep my spirit whole.

Onward, then, I go my way
through all the pain and fear;
Yet, knowing all the live-long day,
my Lord is always near.

So, pilgrim-soldier of the Cross,
while traveling through this land,
Never once forget our Lord
and His loving, nail-pierced hands!

For they will never fail thee!
He is closer than a friend.
And He will always comfort you,
and keep you 'til the end!

It's a Small World (After All!)

I recall my very first mission trip, traveling with Dr. Frank Terry, a minister in the south Georgia area, who took me to Costa Rica and the little village of Cuidad Neilly, located in the southern zone near the Panama border. Our task was to finish the construction of a church which had been started by prior work-teams from the U.S. We were to spend ten days living among the people of that community and sharing our faith with them while working on the community church. There, I would learn one of the greatest lessons in life—WE ARE ALL ONE GREAT BIG COMMUNITY UNDER GOD! It's funny how the world becomes much smaller to us the more we get to know it, and how we all seem to be living in the same "neighborhood."

The people of Cuidad Neilly were shabbily dressed but had hearts of gold. The water was often contaminated, so we had carried pills which killed any contaminants to put in the water which we would drink . The food we were served was very starchy and low in protein, but the folks had somehow survived by the grace of our Lord.

Each night we would celebrate the day's work with the people in their local church building. Oh, how they did enjoy church worship there! The services would often last from two to three hours! After having toiled in the very hot and humid Costa Rican sun all day, those long services would really try our faith, but we were mesmerized by their devotion and loyalty to God. At the close of each service, we would all hug each other and the locals and would listen to their witnesses as well. We soon discovered that we were all of the same persuasion— BROTHERS AND SISTERS IN CHRIST! It made no difference when we worshipped together as to the color of skin or the political beliefs of the two different countries, nor in the difference of language, creeds, or doctrine. We were all ONE IN THE LORD! Several conversions to Christ took place during those ten days, and some of them included fellow team-members! Many of us had our hearts *strangely warmed.*

I will never forget having knelt down at the altar one night with one of those teenage boys. As we both held hands at the altar and prayed for each other, we could not understand the language of the other, but both of us sensed that we were praying together "in the spirit" of our Lord. We were both refreshed when it was over, and I had really become humbled by it all.

My heart yearns for such sincerity of faith here in the U.S. that I witnessed among those simple folk in Costa Rica. I am constantly reminded of people who had very little there, as far as the world's goods are concerned, but who had everything because they had CHRIST in their hearts.

I willingly volunteered my services the following year to return on a mission trip to the Yucatan Peninsula in Mexico where we worked on another new church building. There, before the mission was over, we had made life-long friends with the people of the community because they had felt our concern, care and sincerity of heart. Many there also gave their hearts afresh and anew to Christ. Is it little wonder that I yearn for another opportunity to return to the field of missions in the near future? It is a wonderful opportunity for anyone to grow in grace and to see the Lord at work in other parts of the world.

(I have now been on 68 foreign mission trips across the world, including both Central and South America, the Caribbean, and Europe. I held the position of Coordinator for United Methodist Volunteers in Mission for several years in the South Georgia Annual Conference and' led numerous national trips to hurricane and tornado riddled areas in recovery and restoration attempts.)

Hypocrites Anonymous (H.A.)

Hebrews 10:25:

"Not forsaking the assembling of ourselves together, as the manner of some is; but exhorting one another; and so much the more, as ye see the day approaching."

I recently had a church member criticize the church. Imagine that! This is nothing new in twenty-first century America for we will seemingly criticize anything in which we find the least amount of fault. We are the products of our fathers' bombs and our own nuclear age. We are anxious and prone to frustration, and if things aren't just right, we are ready to criticize and condemn.

At any rate, in my conversation with this member, I asked him to return to church since he had been away for almost five years. He had not been attending church elsewhere, so I was determined to get him active and back in regular worship again.

The member quickly informed me that the church was full of *hypocrites* and that he would not return until it was rid of them.

Well, at this point, I informed him that one more hypocrite wouldn't upset things as they presently were, so he should return.

He then asked me what I meant by my statement. I

gladly informed him that the church sought after perfection in Christ in her present state, and that all of us were really hypocrites because we professed faith in Christ but often lived otherwise. Then I informed him that those who attended regularly were trying to do something about their hypocrisy.

The word from Hebrews reminds us that we are not to forsake the assembling of ourselves together, but should attempt to worship together, for we are made stronger in the Lord when we do so. We should therefore exhort, or teach, and train one another in the faith for the "day of the Lord" is soon approaching.

I'm sure you've heard the old saying that *seven days without Christ makes one w-e-a-k.* Well, friend, it's absolutely true. We cannot and will not survive without Christ being the central figure in our lives on a weekly and daily basis. We need Him and we need each other.

After I assured my friend that one more hypocrite in our church wouldn't upset the applecart, I figured that I really wouldn't see him in church again. I assumed that I had probably turned him off for good and he would not be back in our services. But God has His way of dealing with our weaknesses. I prayed for the man daily, and lo and behold, a few Sundays later, there he was—FRONT and CENTER! He's been a regular attendee since that day, and I give glory to God for turning his heart around.

Let us not forget that we are to assemble ourselves together as often as we can as Christians. We need to lift each other up and add strength where there is weakness, hope where there is hopelessness, vision for those without sight, and love where there is the absence of love.

I'm wondering if perhaps we shouldn't rename the church—HYPOCRITES ANONYMOUS, for we are all hypocrites, but at least we do realize that fact and Christians are trying to do something about it.

From Seattle With Love

It's approximately 3,500 miles from Atlanta, Georgia, to Seattle, Washington, clearly on the other side of the U.S. Roundtrip, it's approximately 7,000 miles total. Try making that trip in only two days!

Some years ago, I discovered one day that my best friend's sister was not doing well and had merely hours to live. She had received a bone marrow transplant at the Fred Hutchinson Cancer Research Center in Seattle, but had been placed on a life-support system afterwards. The transplant had taken several days earlier, but now she had developed a yeast infection in her bloodstream and was not given long to live.

As soon as I heard this news from my friend, I responded by saying, "Let's go!" There was no time to waste if he was to see his sister alive again. I dropped what I was doing, along with other plans for the day, called my wife, Renee, and told her that I was calling Atlanta to get two tickets for my friend and me and did not know when we would be back. We had only three hours to make it to the Atlanta Airport, secure our tickets and go through check-in. We were three and a half hours away, but somehow God shortened that time and we made our flight. I am always amazed at God's timing!

We left Atlanta on that Tuesday afternoon flight and arrived in Seattle (by way of Denver and Portland) an hour too late. She had just died, but the family, knowing that we were on our way, had the hospital staff leave my friend's sister in her room until our arrival. My friend and I were able to see her and to pray with her and the family one last time. I felt that his sister knew our presence.

It was indeed a very solemn trip back to Georgia the following day with our hearts saddened by the event. I had known the young girl since her birth and had watched her grow up to become a beautiful young lady. She had married and was enjoying the time of her life when the cancer struck. Many of her friends and churches in the Albany, Georgia, area had raised countless funds to help the girl and her family fight the cancer. In the process of doing this, the Lord brought many people together and I guess, in a sense, it helped my best friend and me to realize that no matter how serious the event, or how costly it may have been, WE COULD ALWAYS COUNT ON EACH OTHER! We've always been there for each other if and whenever needed, and that means a great deal today in a world that really could seem to care less!

We know that the sister had been told, before we arrived in Seattle, that we were on our way to see her, and we just sensed as we entered her room that she knew our presence.

A few days later I did her eulogy and graveside committal in Albany with a very large crowd of people in attendance. This young lady's life had touched many and it was heartening to see the outpouring of their love and concern.

Jesus reminds us to LOVE ONE ANOTHER, and also to GO THE SECOND MILE with one another if necessary. So, from Seattle, I bring you love—an extraordinary love that can dramatically change this old world through the grace of our Lord Jesus Christ.

A Lesson in Faith

The halls and wards of a major hospital can be very lonely and depressing places at times. There can also be times of elation when one receives good news or when rejoicing occurs over the birth of a healthy child. Hospitals are paradoxical by nature, therefore, filled with both good and bad news. It is the place of the living and the dying. Life and death seemingly mesh together in order to give us a better understanding of and appreciation for life, which we often take for granted until our lives, or those of our family members or friends, are threatened. The latter experience becomes a case-in-point for me to share with you now.

As a minister of the gospel, I have had many experiences with death and dying, both with those struggling to survive day-by-day, and those who bring forth new life by the birth of a child. There have been many happy stories, as well as sad ones. The one I relate now has both characteristics.

The story begins approximately one year after the death of a young man whose courageous actions and beliefs became both an integral part of my life, as well as inspiration in the lives of countless others!

Joseph Arnold Pope, Jr., was a well-loved and ad-
mired young man who had made his way through life, not
taking (as many do), but by giving himself to any cause he
encountered. He had graduated with honors from Georgia
Tech in Atlanta, Georgia, and had a very secure position
as Chief Industrial Engineer with a large Atlanta corpora-
tion where he had worked for several years. He had, as we
generally say, arrived. Life had been good to him, or so it
seemed.

One day Joseph began to notice a gnawing pain in his
lower abdomen and decided to have it checked by his phy-
sician. Through a process of tests, which lasted several
weeks, it was discovered that Joseph had leukemia. Isn't it
strange how things can be going well one day and then, all
of a sudden, life drops a load in your lap such as this!

Plans were immediately made for Joseph to begin a
series of chemotherapy treatments for the leukemia. He
would receive the treatments every seven-weeks during
that first year. He continued to work as much as he could
and to hold on to every thread of hope he could muster.
There were many in his life who gave encouragement and
love to Joseph on a daily basis.

Soon, Joseph began taking further treatments at
Emory University Hospital in Atlanta, and became a very

familiar face on the sixth-floor G-wing of the hospital. This was the ward for all leukemia patients.

Joseph's Sunday School class, having been aware of his disease, became very supportive with fund-raisers, offerings, and individual gifts towards his treatment expenses, at one point raising $6,500 in one week!

From work to a week, two weeks, or a month of hospitalization, Joseph hung in there, fighting for every precious moment of life. He learned an even greater appreciation for life around him, and I can truthfully say that I never once heard Joseph complain of his disease or the pain. I witnessed him in excruciating pain often during that time, but his demeanor would always be lively and hopeful.

Soon, the leukemia ran its course—from remission to hospitalization and treatments, back to remission, and so on. Hope would arrive one day and disappear the next. Joseph seemed to take it all in stride as a mighty warrior faces the heat of battle. But finally, the cancer had its way—the battle was over. Joseph had fought it altogether for approximately four years! There were those who said that he had finally traded in the "thorns of life" for a "crown of glory." He had, in such a short number of years, lived far longer than most people would live in seventy! He was only thirty-three, but the courage and faith he showed us throughout that trying ordeal will always be a memorial to us of that great young man.

The halls of Emory University Hospital, the doctors and nurses who cared for Joseph, the many patients he gave hope to through his strong faith, and the lives of those who knew and loved him and his vibrant witness, will always remind me of Joseph's faith.

Joseph Arnold Pope, Jr. always looked upon death as a venture into a new life, one complete with Christ without the suffering and pain one experiences here. He took the good with the bad and made the utmost out of his short, abbreviated life, thus giving hope to all of us who remain. We, too, can make it if we will press forward in faith, regardless of what we may encounter.

Joseph's spirit remains with us today, leading, guiding and urging us to "fight the good fight" and to win the victory.

As you retire tonight, please remember to pray for the countless numbers of those who walk the halls of our hospital wards and for those who lie upon those beds day-by-day suffering and hoping for just one more day or one more hour of life.

God's Great Sacrificial Love

We had chickens in a pen out back when I was growing up in south Georgia. We picked up the eggs each morning and that would be part of our breakfast. We would also pick out one of our largest hens and would kill it, clean it, and serve it up with dumplings and dressing for special occasions such as Easter, Christmas, etc. One of my special duties daily was to see to it that the chickens were fed. I enjoyed that job and could oftentimes be found talking to the chickens as I fed them. Many of them I had given names to, and several had become so familiar with me that they would approach me and allow me to hold them like a pet!

I'll never forget one cold winter when the chicken coup caught on fire and we lost a lot of those old hens and their biddies (baby chicks). The coup was enclosed with a high, wire fence, and we couldn't get them all out when the fire started. Many of them were too startled and would run under the feeders to get away from the fire.

After the fire was out, we began cleaning up and searching for any survivors. It was like World War III in that hen house! I remember stumbling over a blackened heap on the ground, too charred to really tell what it was at first glance. I kicked it over and out ran six beautiful little chicks! The heap had been the mother hen who had opened up her wings and had drawn her chicks underneath those wings to save them from the fire! In the process of saving her chicks, she had sacrificed her life. Six little chicks would continue to live and to produce, but now the mother was gone. Her life became a living sacrifice for her chicks.

How often we are reminded in the scriptures that God is like that mother hen with us. He loves us with a compassionate, sacrificial love. He loved us so much, in fact, that He sent His only Son, Jesus, to die on a cruel, old, rugged cross for our sins and for the sins of the world. In essence, Christ took the world under His great wings of love and kept sin from destroying us. He offers us eternal life if we will only put our faith in Him and believe in Him and trust our lives to His constant care. God's great sacrificial love is available today to any and all who will call upon His name and believe.

In The Shadow
of My Father

I walked behind a man today . . .
not just any man,
but a man who had worked the good earth
for years with his bare hands—
calloused and wrinkled with years;
a man who had fought for four years
on foreign soil in the "Great War,"
worked the turpentine-sap from southern pines,
ran a feed-mill and had lost
at both love and war!

I walked behind a man who had
tasted the "good ole days"
when things had seemed much
easier than today;
a man who had taught me much about
such things as hog-killings,
how to hunt squirrel in the woods,
how to mend fences,
call a cow,
plow a mule,
build a crib to store our harvest.

That man showed me how to
catch a ball,
catch a fish,
and chase the moon!
He filled my head with more dreams
than I can begin to recall.
He laughed with me,
cried with me,
hurt with me,

suffered with me, and then—
He died!

How could I have ever imagined
that a body once so active,
so strong,
so immortal to me as a child,
would now lie there so still,
so cold,
so lifeless,
so mortal?

There is
and always will be now
a great void in my life that
no other human being could ever fill.

I must be thankful though
for all of the good things—
the dreams,
the visions,
the hopes and longings
that he once instilled in me
during those few, brief years of life.

As I think on these things,
I am reminded that I, too,
will one day face my own mortality
and know the mysteries of death.

But today,
for these precious moments in time,
I must be as my father was—
resolute, immovable, strong
for there is one
who walks behind me in my shadow,

and I must not fail
to pass along to him
the heritage of the past;
For one day,
in the yet, unforeseen future,
hopefully one will walk behind him—
tender,
young,
unlearned,
and seeking the mysteries of life.

I must be firm,
diligent as an eagle,
yet, loving,
kind,
and full of grace.

Still, even today,
my mind goes back to 1957
on God's little acre,
when I,
barefoot and dirty-faced
child of only six,
walked those long furrows of
freshly plowed earth
behind a GIANT of a man—
my father,
and that old beast of burden.
There, I felt that all the world
and everything in it was
completely under dad's control.

Just today,
As I turned and looked behind me,
I saw in the eyes of my own son
my eyes as a child!

I saw my father again,
face-to-face,
and caught a wee small glimpse
of yesterday
and tomorrow!

This Day From Slumber

(In Memory of George Washington Ennis:
March 30, 2000)

This day, from slumber, I awoke
as any day before,
to hear the birds in carol sing
outside my kitchen door.

I listened quite intently to
the call of Nature ring;
loud and clear, its clarion call—
I heard the angels sing.

Softly, they did beckon me
to journey with them today.
So, faithfully, I followed them
to Heaven's grand stairway.

What wondrous beauty I beheld
inside those golden gates!
And yet, my spirit doth now grieve
for loved ones who still wait.

Still I am comforted to know
that one day they shall see
this wondrous place of beauty rare
beyond tranquility.
When you shall hear the birds sweet call,
and watch the squirrels at play,
know full-well that I am with thee—
just look for me today!

Mosaics of My Life

Others have shaped my life,
for no man is an island.
Others have impacted my thoughts
for good or evil.
This pyramid of influence
has spanned eons of time to create
generation after generation
of those who walk upon these shores,
following new and old paradigms.
Whether by choice or not,
I am part of those who have
preceded me;
dreamers and actors upon the stage
who sought better ways to
express themselves.
I find that we are each part
of the other,
no more—no less.
The picture of my life is expressed
by those who have journeyed with
and behind me.
Their voices speak volumes.
I listen and learn from their wisdom,
their mistakes;
clay in the Potter's hands.
And yet, I am a very unique specimen,
loaded with my own D.N.A.
Even that has been given by those
of my past!
Here, I weave intricate patterns, mosaics
of both past, present and future.

This Immortality

It lurks in shadows of one's soul,
and wakens truth in me.
It lingers through the longest day—
This immortality.

'Round every corner, every bend,
Wherever my heart leads,
I cannot escape its calling—
This immortality.

It beckons midst the longest days,
From it, I'm never free.
It walks beside me in the way—
This immortality.

I shall not fear its presence,
My friend, in death, to me;
For one day it will take me home—
This immortality!

Great God, Almighty is He

There was darkness in my valley,
I was blinded by my shame;
Until the voice of Jesus
Called out my very name!
Friend, if you are thirsty,
And need light unto your soul,
Open up your heart to Me
And I will make you whole!

He sent manna from the heavens
To feed my weary soul.
Water from a desert rock,
Flowing free and bold.
He took away my every sin,
His blood now covers me.
He's the Lily of my Valley,
Great God, Almighty is He!

If you've been drifting in sorrow,
And can't find your way back home,
Just turn your eyes to Jesus
And you'll never be alone.
He'll be your friend, companion,
Your constant guide He'll be.
So open up your heart to Him,
And let Him set you free!

The Life Line

(For David Hinson—Friend for Life)

They were all out at sea when his son fell overboard,
and the son's best friend fell in too.
With only one life line, the father made a choice
As to which one he would throw the line to.
His son was a Christian, an example of faith,
But the best friend had never been saved.
He knew that his son would be taken to heaven,
So he pulled the best friend from the waves!

What a heartbreaking scene as his son disappeared
Far beneath that old wild, raging sea!
Only one could he save on that fateful day,
And that best friend just happened to be ME!

It was an old rugged cross where a precious son died,
On that fateful and memorable day;
When God, the dear Father, sacrificed His Son
To take all my sins away!

Now, with an old dog-eared Bible, I stand every week
And I preach about Jesus and me;
And how a father's great love pulled me from my despair,
And how Jesus once saved even me!
There are many lost souls drowning in life's sea,
And only one life line is thrown.
Take it, my friend, and be saved today,
And soon you'll be going home!

The Plan of Salvation

"That if you confess with your mouth, 'Jesus is Lord,' and believe in your heart that God raised him from the dead, you will be saved" (Romans 10:9).

Let me make this as clear as possible without any theological debate. God is seeking a personal relationship with you through His son, Jesus Christ. Follow these simple steps if you desire new life in Christ today.

1. Admit your need of Christ. Admit that you are a sinner and that you desire the salvation Christ offers.

2. Repent of your sins and open your heart to Christ now.

3. Trust in your heart and believe that Christ died for you on that old rugged Cross and that He rose again from the dead.

4. Right now in prayer, invite the Lord Jesus Christ to come into your heart and to control your life through His wonderful Holy Spirit. He will become Lord and Savior of your soul at this point.

5. Begin living the righteous life before Christ. Share your faith with others, and grow in the Spirit.

Finally, I invite you to pray the following prayer in earnest, seeking the fullness of God in your life:

DEAR LORD JESUS:

I am a sinner and I seek Your forgiveness. Lord, I believe that You died for my sins on the cross, and I want to turn from my sins now to You. I invite You into my heart and life and ask that You make of me a new creation in Your image and likeness. Help me, Lord, to trust in You as my personal Savior and to follow You all of my life.

In Jesus' Name I pray—AMEN.

Now that you have completed this simple plan of salvation, the key is to share your faith and experience with another person; be it your pastor, best friend, co-worker or even a stranger. This will enable your faith to grow tremendously. The more you share what has happened in your life will help lead others into the way. God bless you on your new journey!

"Mr. Mac"

In the small south Georgia town where I grew up, there lived a legend in the person of Daniel Lee McGlaughlin. Everyone there called him affectionately, *Mr. Mac*. Today, there is a baseball field in Helena, Georgia, dedicated to his memory, and rightfully so. Mr. Mac was always coaching baseball and helping young boys learn to play the "game of life" (as he called it!) through his gracious witness. He was also our City Clerk for many years.

I was not born into a wealthy family, by any stretch of imagination. It was always difficult for my family to make ends meet, but somehow we managed. My mom worked at two jobs to help my father keep things going and also took on sewing and ironing on the side for neighbors.

I remember signing up for Little League baseball when I reached eligibility and met Mr. Mac for the first time. A couple of boys and I had been to City Hall that day to sign up, and there he was, sitting behind his big desk, looking larger than life itself! As far as I was concerned, he could have been President of the United States.

We began practices a few days later, and Mr. Mac took to my abilities right away. He tried me at several positions and finally decided that "catcher" was where he needed me most. He was constantly bragging on me and my abilities to catch and to throw to second base. My hitting was "tweeners" (between second base and first, and shortstop and third). I was never able to hit home runs, but he gladly accepted my ability to hit the gaps.

The day of our first game (which would be that night), I went up to City Hall to ascertain what time we needed to be at the fields in McRae. Mr. Mac told me to be there at 6:00 p.m., and then noticed that I still had on my holey tennis shoes borrowed from one of my brothers. He asked me if my folks had not bought me some cleats (baseball shoes) to play in that night, and I told him that they were going to buy some but the money had been really tight at the moment. Mr. Mac knew my family well and knew the many difficulties we had been through.

He took me into his storage room and said, "Son, if you're going to be my starting catcher tonight, you can't play that position without some cleats." He picked up a box, after sizing my feet with his eyes, and asked that I open the box and try on the shoes inside.

When I opened the box, with amazement, I saw a beautiful pair of black baseball shoes with white stripes down each side! It was the only box of shoes left, for most of the other kids had already purchased theirs days before.

With a great sense of humility, I slipped the shoes on and laced them up, realizing that they were just a bit too big on me, but I never once let Mr. Mac know it. When I walked around that room with my new shoes on, Mr. Mac spoke again.

"Son, just think of those shoes as a special gift to a boy that I believe in! You're gonna be a good player and make me very proud of you. Always remember that when you're wearing those shoes, you have to do your best. And remember also that I believe in you. You'll have a chance one day to do the same for someone else."

Not knowing what he was referring to, I thanked him and rushed home with my new shoes on and dressed in my uniform for the game that night, a full six hours early. That night I played my heart out for Mr. Mac. It would be that way for the next four years of Little League, every game, giving my very best.

After Little League, I moved up to Pony League. Since we only had one team, Mr. Mac was again my coach. He chose me again as his starting catcher and I played that position for him the next four years as we traveled across south Georgia playing other city teams. We

were good—very good—and usually won every tourna-
ment we entered. Mr. Mac's enthusiasm and constant be-
lief in "his" boys was the reason behind our many victo-
ries. We were probably just a mediocre team at best, but
Mr. Mac had us believing that we were always the very
best. We all played well-beyond our abilities for the man
who put his faith in us.

Mr. Mac had always been somewhat handicapped.
His vision was very poor, but he never let it show. He was
the kind of man who was always rising above his handi-
caps and teaching his boys to do the same.

To every boy who ever passed through that Little
League and Pony League program, Mr. Mac is still quite a
legend and always will be. The field in Helena, Georgia,
dedicated in his memory, is a tribute far greater to me than
Yankee Stadium or Turner Field in Atlanta. It was there
on that field of dreams that an old man taught a lot of wet-
back, inexperienced farm boys how to become men! He
taught us faith, trust, loyalty and devotion in the midst of
oftentimes insurmountable odds. Many of "his" boys are
now baseball coaches, teachers, lawyers, doctors, and
yes—even ministers! Funny, isn't it, what a pair of new
baseball shoes can do for a little boy of nine!

Before I retired from coaching Little League in several different cities, I had spent twenty-six years giving back the joy I discovered from my tutelage with Mr. Mac. I have sought to instill in each of "my" boys the things Mr. Mac taught us.

Just a few years back now, I bought a new pair of baseball shoes and gave them to a little migrant-Mexican boy who played on my Little League team in Reidsville, Georgia. After seeing him put those shoes on at practice, I felt it somewhat strange to suddenly realize that HE was my starting catcher! In some small way, the spirit of Mr. Mac continues to live on.

I remember that day when I received my first set of cleats and Mr. Mac saying, "Son, you'll have a chance one day to do the same for someone else."

And so the legend lives on . . .

The Cart-Man's Inspiration

I knew a man once who had no legs. He lived alone, but never once allowed his handicap to become an excuse. He had built a little wooden flat that he could sit on and had installed rollers underneath the flat to motivate himself. He designed special cups for his hands which enabled him to push himself and his cart down the road. Each morning, very early, one could see him along the side of the highway, pushing himself two miles through heavy traffic to town where he would then join a men's fellowship time at a local coffee shop. There, he would serve as great inspiration to others who knew his plight, and admired his great effort. He never once allowed anyone to show pity towards him.

This man was determined to be the very best that he could be, despite having no legs. It was always great inspiration for me to see him on his little cart, wheeling himself down the highway. I always thought that if he could do that with no legs, how much more should I be able to do with two!

You have probably heard the old saying, "I used to complain because I had no shoes, until I saw a man who had no feet." Isn't that just like the majority of us, constantly complaining about what we lack, instead of realizing the great blessing in what we DO have and using those for the ultimate good?

What handicap are you complaining about today? I invite you to turn that handicap into a blessing. Put it to use and show others in the process how they, too, can turn handicaps into blessings. Your attitude, of course, will have to change in order to do this, but you can do it.

Remember this, "Nothing ventured, nothing gained." And again, "If you aim at nothing—you're sure to hit it!" God bless each of you.

Dynamic Living for
Dangerous Times

A friend shared a cartoon with me recently in which a man is lying on the couch in a psychiatrist's office. He is evidently pouring out his soul to the doctor as he looks around the office at all the diplomas and shelves of books. He is in complete awe with what his doctor has accomplished.

Suddenly, something in one corner of the room catches the man's attention. He looks in horror and complete surprise for the wallpaper is coming unglued and is beginning to curl-up. Underneath the wallpaper, the man can see that the books and diplomas are actually nothing more than clever pictures printed on the wallpaper!

There he is on the doctor's couch, desperately needing help, but realizing that he has been opening up his life to a fraud! In the last and final frame, there is no caption—just the man's expression of disappointment, and you understand his predicament.

What do we do when our little secure world begins to roll-up around the edges, revealing the bare sheetrock and walls behind it? When those trusted answers are finally revealed as NO answers at all? How do we get beyond the wallpaper of our existence and move beyond the façade?

Today's modern electronic world offers you instant and complete gratification for only $19.95, *plus shipping and handling!* All you have to do is order their product and you'll find instant joy. Isn't it strange that not everyone buys Anthony Robbins' "get-rich-quick-schemes?" There are products today which promise to run errands for you, increase your self-confidence, assure you happiness, and even conquer your worst fears. All of that, of course, for a price!

Well then, how to we get beyond the wallpaper, the façade, and really begin living the dynamic life we're all seeking? The answer is really quite simple—the power is within YOU. According to the electronic world, you are nothing more than a mere machine which responds to self-gratification, greed and selfishness. You are nothing more than a bundle of appetites seeking satisfaction.

Let me share some important news with you at this point: the world **cannot**, nor ever **will be** able to completely satisfy you! That has to come from deep within each person's soul.

Think about this for a moment. If those commercials are right, then we should be able to smoke one of their cigarettes and be eternally satisfied. Fact of the matter is that they purposefully put TWENTY in each pack, knowing that you will want another one, and then another one to satisfy the craving that is created from smoking. It's an endless cycle and companies base their entire future on your addiction to their products.

Another case-in-point: why is it that beer manufacturers make "six-packs" and "cases" of beer? Simply because they know that after you've had the first one you'll want a second, and a third . . . Before you know it you're hooked! Nothing more than a mindless idiot who proceeds to wreck his home, his family, his career and everything he touches in life. Is this *dynamic* living? I'm afraid not. We've all been sold a fraud! When the wallpaper finally starts to peel, we begin to see everything from an entirely different perspective. The world *cannot* satisfy you. Only YOU have the power and the ability within to change. Tap into that hidden resource and discover the new life. The secret is found in the human heart.

Let me share in closing four keys to dynamic living that have helped me tremendously.

1. **Begin where you are with people you know**. Develop their friendship; encourage their care, concern and love. Start small with perhaps one or two of your closest friends. Bring them into you life. Listen to their ad-

vice. Seek their counsel. Share a part of your life with them.

2. **Keep Going!** Do not allow discouragement to let you down. See it simply as another roadblock that can be maneuvered around. Keep the momentum in your life going as well. Keep moving! It is, after all, the rock which never moves in the stream of life which catches all of the proverbial moss.

3. **Be positive, hopeful and practical**. Never turn into a sour-puss, showing a negative or judgmental attitude. Think positively. Be filled with hope, but remember to keep your life practical.

4. **Keep your eyes open, your mind alert, and your courage unshakeable!** Be strong and confident, dynamic and exuberant about life and living. Get busy by starting today.

Break Out of the Rut

Stuck in a rut? Can't seem to get out of that regular routine? Want to make a change but something seems to keep holding you back? If so, then I have some good news for you. Try applying the following seven directives to your life and see what difference they can make.

1. **Begin assuming responsibility for your own life.** Stop fretting over how and why things have gone sour for you. Take charge of the present and refocus your energies. Become responsible for each of your actions and re-actions. Don't just be a "responder" to events and occurrences that happen in your life. Act BEFORE things happen. PLAN, PLAN, PLAN and then WORK YOUR PLAN. Be the instigator for the things you desire to happen.

2. **Believe in the possibility that you CAN change.** Never settle for what others think of you. Believe that you can change and then go for it today. Break out of that mold. Move beyond your present state and test the waters of life. You will never succeed as long as you're stuck in that rut!

3. **Clarify.** What are the things you really need at the present? Are they clear to you and your vision, or are there other less important matters clouding the issues? Try simplifying your life—cut out the "junk" and clarify your goals and directions. Catch a new vision of who you are and what you hope to accomplish in this life. After the fog has lifted, everything will be much clearer and more focused.

4. **Stop Worrying!** Worry has perhaps taken more lives than many other causes combined, simply because people allow such worries to complicate an already complicated life. Stop worrying as to what other people will say about you when you start to get your life in order. Worry is the product of indecision, frustration and confusion. Do not allow its ill-effects to put you in an even deeper rut than you're already in. Rise above your worries and conquer them instead.

5. **Stop waiting for ideal circumstances.** How true it is that, "Nothing would be done at all if a person waited until he could do it so well that no one could find fault with it." I'm not certain who it was that first coined that phrase, but it makes perfect sense, doesn't it? Stop

trying to perfect everything in your life before you start making it happen for you. Others will pass you by if you keep waiting on perfection.

6. **Step out boldly in FAITH.** Faith is the belief in some "one" or some "thing." It does, however, go a step further. Faith is only alive and active when we put it into motion. You must have faith in yourself, your abilities, your skills, and the many possibilities for your life. You must believe in yourself and your capabilities before you can begin to make progress towards a successful new life. Once you have that faith in operation, then step out boldly, dramatically, and with confidence to achieve your quest.

7. **Do it NOW!** Do not wait or procrastinate! Whatever you desire to do, do it NOW! Today, this very moment in time, is really all that you have. Make the most of it, my friend!

The Gift That Lasts

Troubadour's in platelet labs,
Sacrificial giving;
Saints who give themselves away
To help the barely living.
Sterile tubes inserted,
Vessels punctured, gift begins;
Now to aid the one who's dying,
Dear and precious loving friend!

Blood now flows through plastic tubes,
Circulating and returning;
Filtered platelets drawn apart,
Given to the one who's yearning.
And so it goes day in and out,
The hope remains therein
That what they're giving of themselves
Will bring new life again!

For the Lab-techs and the Nurses,
God has touched you with His Grace.
Just remember to be gentle
As you look upon each face.
For when you see their sacrifice,
Remember God above—
Once gave His precious Son, the Christ,
Upon a tree in love.

God bless you all for what you do,
The donors and technicians;
For what you do is marked above
In God's Book of Decision!

Never falter, never fail,
Always equal to the task;
And hopefully, what you do today,
Will be THE GIFT THAT LASTS!

God of the Sparrow

God of the sparrow, who lifts up the fallen,
God of the child who has lost his way . . .
God of all mercy, whose tender compassion,
Heals me and cleanses my sins away!

God of the morning, so bright and blessed,
God of the night, Who ruleth above . . .
God of the noonday and all that is in it,
Guide me, Jehovah, and fill me with love.

God of the harvest, bountiful, plenty,
Ever supplying my constant need.
God of our Savior, Earth's blessed rapture,
On thy dear Word, Lord, I'll always feed!

Strength and Comfort
(For All Saints Day)

When those storms of life prevaileth,
When the tides of change may rise,
I will give thee strength and courage;
In my bosom you'll abide.

Though this life is filled with terror,
Never fear for I'll be there.
I will honor thee with Spirit,
And my gracious loving care.

And when time on earth has ended,
I will take thee safely home.
I'll give comfort to thy loved ones;
They shall never feel alone.

I shall send my holy angels,
They will bring thee home to me;
On their wings of peace and comfort,
In my kingdom you shall be!

For *All Saints* who from their labor,
Look upon us from above,
We will celebrate their presence
With unending Christian love!

The Imperfect Opal

An opal is a very unique gem, comprised of sand and silica, and is a product of the desert. It has tiny little fissures which allow air inside, thus giving off a refraction of light with lovely hues. When it is held in a warm hand, it will show off its luster and beauty. However, if it is placed in a cold, dark place, it will quickly lose its luster. Some have referred to it as the "Lamp of Fire" and have said that the breath of God is within it. The fissures are actually imperfections, but they give the gem life!

We are relatively like opals, replete with various imperfections and flaws. If kept to ourselves, we become nothing more than cold, hardened stones. When given love and care, however, we become alive and vibrant again, full of life. Even our imperfections and flaws can be turned into a beautiful semblance of our Lord Jesus Christ if we are loved and will allow ourselves to be loved.

In each pastorate over the last thirty-eight years, I have made it a point to be a "hugging" pastor to all willing members. In fact, I have become known as the "Hugging Preacher" in many such pastorates. I recall one member a few years back who was very shy and actually refused to hug me on my first attempt. Being one who would never force a hug on a person, I took note not to hug that person. In the months to come, however, several events occurred in her life that would serve to transform her attitude. Following an evening worship service, I gave an altar call and she came down to me and gave me the biggest hug I had ever received! Surprised, to say the least, she simply told me that the "Lord had asked her to do that." She is now one of the first to hug me whenever I return to that particular church. She also has a new and very becoming gleam in her eyes because her love of Christ has grown immeasurably. Strange what new life a simple hug can bring in someone's life!

The church is comprised of losers, flawed with the sins of this life, needing God's abundant pardon and love. We are like the opal, desiring to be loved and held by someone who cares. The world doesn't care—that's simply its nature—but the church should care!

Christmas Memories

(Written by Renee D. Cravey)

"Wake up, Daddy. Wake up, Mama. Santa's come!" I exclaimed that each Christmas morning as a child. Christmas was always an exciting time at our house. Our family was so rich with love that I was grown before I realized that we were poor. I guess that somehow I knew my parents didn't have a lot of extra money for Christmas presents, so I never asked for very much. However, there were always gifts we didn't ask for underneath the tree on Christmas morning.

One year I remember going with my sister and our daddy to look for a Christmas tree. After trekking deep into the woods on our farm, we came back with a spindly little pine tree. Daddy either made a stand or put it in a bucket of some kind; I don't remember which. I just know it stood and filled the house with the sweet smell of pine. We drove the short distance across the creek to my uncle's house and borrowed a string of big bulb Christmas lights, as his children were older and they weren't going to decorate a tree. It seems like we had a package of tinsel. I don't remember ornaments of any kind. We were so proud of that little tree. It made Christmas "official."

Another Christmas, there was a bike—just one bike for both my sister and me. It would never have occurred to either of us to have expected *two* bikes. Since we were only sixteen months apart in age, we knew how to take turns and share. That was instilled in us at an early age.

Every year a few of the children at our tiny country church would dress up like Mary, Joseph, shepherds, wise men, and angels and re-enact the Christmas story for the congregation. Someone would provide the all-important doll for the baby Jesus. There would be a huge tree covered in shiny colored balls and other ornaments. Santa would make a visit to distribute gifts and fruit after the play. I'll never forget the time that I missed my daddy right before Santa's arrival. Of course, I recognized him, but never let on that I did!

Those were some of the happiest moments of my childhood. My daddy and mama gave us gifts at Christmas, but the best gift was the love that we experienced not only at Christmas but each and every day. God loves each of us, just as my parents loved us. He gave us, His children, the very best gift for Christmas—His only Son, Jesus Christ.

Pacific Garden Missions

A radio dramatization of my early life was recently aired over the radio for an entire week beginning on September 12, 2010 by Chicago's *Pacific Garden Missions.* An earlier one was aired in 1986, also for a week. The program is broadcast around the world more than 10,000 times each week on over 2,200 radio outlets in eight different languages. This recent program is #3113 and you may go to the website and listen to it at the following address:

www.unshackled.org

Go to 09.12.10 for the Charles Cravey Classic

The Pacific Garden Missions has been in operation since 1877 and has been a refuge for many weary, struggling pilgrims. The Mission provides food, shelter, and clothing, as well as medical and dental care to numerous indigents each year. The radio broadcasts are dramatized by the staff and produced on radio throughout the year seeking to minister to as many lost souls as possible. They provide in-house counseling and spiritual care, offering the answer to broken lives—life through faith in Jesus Christ.

The Mission is located on South Canal Street in Chicago, Illinois, and is a lighthouse for souls lost on life's troubling seas. It is a non-profit organization and the largest such organization in the north-central states. To read about the mission, go to www.pgm.org. Donations are welcomed and greatly appreciated.

This "Charles Cravey Classic" deals with a life of poverty and delinquency, and has reached out to many young people struggling to find their way through the maze of life. I am so thankful that my book agent sent the Mission a copy of my first published book, *Through the Eye of a Needle*, back in the early 1980s to make this presentation possible.

The segment will be aired many more times in the coming years over radio stations worldwide. These take place on a recurring basis in order to get the word of Christ and hope out to a lost generation. Pray for its continued success!

Midnight in the Garden of Gethsemane

(Please read John 18:1-10 for the full story)

It was midnight in the Garden of Gethsemane. Jesus had drawn apart from his disciples to pray there following the Last Supper with them in Jerusalem earlier in the evening. He knew that it would only be moments away from his arrest by the Chief Priests and Roman soldiers, so it was here that he uttered that beautiful prayer, "Not my will, but thine be done." His time on earth was drawing to a close, and the agony of Calvary loomed ever so heavy before him.

Jesus had just met with his disciples for a meal and had tried to explain to them what was to happen but their minds were filled with earthly things. How could he possibly describe the Father's Will to a band of fishermen, carpenters, tax collectors and basket-weavers? They could not possibly comprehend the fullness of the future events which would occur. Even at dinner, the disciples had started an argument among themselves at the table over who would sit beside Jesus when the new kingdom he spoke of arrived. Petty little things, at a moment in which Jesus was facing the ultimate!

We can see much of ourselves in those disciples, can't we? They were human in every possible sense of the word. Hopefully, they would band themselves together when the time came to carry on the ministry Jesus had started among them. But for now, they were letting their selfishness show.

Jesus had taken Peter, James, and the "beloved" John, three of his most trusted disciples, into the Garden with him while he prayed. They were to keep watch, yet fell asleep on the job! Jesus reprimands them and asks why they could not watch for *just* one hour! It is sad to know how weak are those we trust the most. People whom we count on daily often surprise us and let us down when we need them the most.

At any rate, the hour was late (around midnight). Jesus had finished his agonizing prayer when the Chief Priests and Roman guards entered the garden. Judas, one of the twelve disciples, had been to the Priests and had sold Jesus to them for an agreement of 30 pieces of silver. His sign would be to plant a kiss on the cheek of the one called Jesus whenever the guards arrived, signifying the one to be arrested.

With Judas' dirty deed accomplished, Malchus (the personal servant of the High Priest, Caiaphas) takes Jesus by the arm to arrest him. Trusty old Peter, always contentious, pulls out his sword and begins swinging it in all directions, finally landing it on the right ear of Malchus, severing that ear and it falls to the grassy hillside of Gethsemane. Peter is quickly rebuked by Jesus for his act of anger and cruelty and told to put down his sword. Peter was reluctant, but does what the Lord commands.

What happens next is what many have described as "the little miracle before the BIG one." "The Big One" is a reference to the resurrection of Christ. In Jesus' state of mind, facing the cross, he realizes what has just happened to Malchus, a lowly guard. Why would he even be concerned about this Roman? Are the Romans not enemies of his people? Yet, Jesus bends down in the darkness of the garden, finds the bloody ear of Malchus, and then puts it back in its place on the head of Malchus, completely healed!

So many times I have read over this passage and completely skipped right over this little miracle; but to me, it has become a BIG miracle to remind me of how much Jesus cares about all people, even this little Roman guard in the garden. There was no sterile operating room, no sutures, no anesthesia—simply the touch of the Master's hand that healed Malchus' ear. There were no bright lights shining to help Jesus to see what he was doing; simply his touch healed Malchus. What a wonderful story!

Let's imagine that Malchus began his day with the regular routine of kissing his wife and children before leaving for guard duty at the temple. He had stood there for hours, sword in hand, and had kept watch over the people entering and leaving. At lunch, he had a break with his fellow guards and possibly discussed the politics of Jerusalem. At quitting time, he had been asked to stay on late for an entourage to Gethsemane that night to arrest someone important. He had a chance now, he felt, to prove himself worthy of being appointed as a commander, so he agreed to go.

As a band, the group crossed over the Kidron Valley to Gethsemane carrying torches to light the way. They found the three disciples and Jesus and surrounded them. When confronted, Judas immediately greeted them and planted the infamous kiss on the cheek of Jesus. Peter realizes that the group is there to arrest Jesus, so he draws his sword and attacks Malchus, severing that ear. I would venture to guess that Malchus had a change of heart after the healing of his ear and perhaps followed Jesus the rest of his life. This man, he thought, was different than all the rest. He REALLY cared for people.

Surely, we will have mixed feelings about this story. Jesus condemns Peter while we want to praise his actions. Peter drew his sword to protect Jesus from harm, but wasn't it this same Peter who had earlier fallen asleep while supposedly keeping watch for Jesus as He prayed? Wasn't this the same Peter who would later, the following day, deny having known Jesus three times in the city streets of Jerusalem? Why do we so quickly condone the actions of Peter in the garden when we know how wavering his faith was? Could it be that we also see ourselves in him?

Compare, if you will, the two actions of Peter and Jesus. Peter's action came about hastily with anger towards the hungry mob. Jesus' action was filled with compassion for even a centurion guard who had been injured. Oil and water—the two simply do not mix. Jesus knew His time was near, but Peter had no inclination of it. He had ignored most of the conversations at the dinner table that evening, for his main concern had been over who would sit in the seats of honor when the new kingdom arrived. Had he listened carefully to Christ, he would have been aware of the coming events.

I do not blame Peter for I feel his humanity. He did what most of us would have done; he tried to protect the Lord against all odds. Yet, it would be some time later before he would realize and understand the words of Jesus.

Many of us are like Malchus in this story. We're carrying out our duties and responsibilities, trying to do the best we can with life when, all of a sudden, someone throws a curve ball into the mix.

I began this discourse by stating that it was midnight in the Garden of Gethsemane. Let's talk a bit about the midnight of one's soul in relationship to the curve balls that come into our lives. Midnight is that place half-way between the darkness and dawn. Mentally, it is a decision to be made, a moment in time which seems endless when we must step forward or go back, when everything hinges upon whatever happens next. It's Jonah in the belly of the whale; David standing before the giant, Goliath; Jesus in the Garden. We've all been there at some point in time. It's "crunch" time!

King David succinctly said it in that beautiful twenty-third Psalm: "Yea, though I walk through the valley of the shadow of death . . ." That valley can be related to the "midnight" of our souls.

I recall so vividly standing in the waiting room of a major hospital with a young lady's family discussing the alternatives and decisions that needed to be made. For weeks the young lady had been on a life-support system with no progress. The physician had given the family two choices: (1) leave her on the machine and hope for recovery against all odds, or (2) remove the machine from her and allow her to die with dignity. The physician had told them that she had no chance of survival if the machine was removed. Midnight!

Oh, the great agony I saw in the faces of those family members! This was to be a decision they would have to live with for the rest of their lives. The father finally asked that we pray together and so we did, standing there in one big circle in the corridor of that busy hospital. We prayed that God would give the family direction and peace in their decisions. Following the prayer, we all experienced the greatest imaginable calm .

The father spoke first, then the mother, and finally her brother and sister. They were all in agreement—the life support system would be disconnected and they would allow their loved one to die with dignity. Midnight. Irreversible decisions. Setting one's hands to the plow and not looking back. "Yea, though I walk through the valley of the shadow of death . . ."

It was over within a few hours. We were all gathered

around her when she peacefully breathed her last breath. I prayed the prayer of committal while we all stood in a circle around her bed. Indescribable peace entered that room. God's great presence was felt by everyone there. Following our prayer, we looked out the windows and the dawn was just beginning to break. What a beautiful sight! Joy comes in the morning!

What Jesus must have experienced that night in the garden has to be indescribable, but we can all relate to Him. We've walked through those dark valleys of the soul, made those tough decisions, and have experienced the joy that morning brings when the peace of God enters our hearts.

Peter was also having his own midnight experience. How does he respond to the reprimand of Jesus, the one whom he has faithfully left all for and has followed the past three years? Now, he has been shamed for his quick and thoughtless actions. Yet, Peter becomes the "Rock," the solid foundation upon which the early church was built. He could have so easily abandoned Jesus at that point and stammered away in anger, but he remained and learned from the Master another important lesson in life.

And then there is Malchus and his garden experience

(Luke 221:51). What happened to Malchus had to be life transforming. I can see him standing at the foot of the cross the following day with tears in his eyes as he watches his new-found Savior being crucified. I can hear him telling everyone in town about his right ear and how it was miraculously healed by the Galilean in the garden the night before. I see him as a great leader in the early church, crossing the boundaries of his former faith and his new faith in Christ. Perhaps he became one of the early pastors, a great lay leader of the people, or even a mission-ary! Whatever happened, we can assume that his life was never the same, for he had been touched and healed by the Master.

Are you experiencing midnight in the garden of your soul? Oh, my dear friend, there is someone there with you who longs to hold you, love you, and impart His blessed peace to you. Turn it over, turn it ALL over to Jesus right now without delay, and He will see you through.

Servanthood

"If"

If I can stop one heart from breaking
I shall not live in vain;
If I can ease one life the aching
Or cool one pain,
Or help one fainting robin
Unto his nest again,
I shall not live in vain.

- *Emily Dickinson*

In this very poignant verse by Dickinson, we find purpose and a simplistic meaning for life: to do something constructive, meaningful, and timeless for others. What is life if it is not spent reaching out and sharing our lives with others? Weary is the person who spends every waking hour in pursuit of self. We actually "find" ourselves when we are immersed in service to others.

A friend came to see me in my study some years ago, very distraught and downtrodden. He was a very successful businessman by all standards, yet he was missing a key ingredient in his life. He had spent thousands of dollars in seeking out psychiatrists, therapists, and others in the health field in an attempt to find inner peace. It had continued to be elusive for him. He was now at the point of desperation when we talked that day. He explained how he had "arrived" in the business world and had quickly climbed the ladder of success to a position of authority. He had achieved the ultimate level in his field of expertise, yet he lacked an essential ingredient in his life and had visited me for possible help.

Immediately, I asked him about his faith. He said that it had been some time (actually months) since he last attended worship in his church, for he had to do a lot of his work at home on the weekends.

I asked if he still believed in the power of God to save him and to bring new meaning to his brokenness. He answered affirmatively but was somewhat hesitant at that point to move further into our conversation. I prodded him further, however.

As our conversation grew, I discovered that he had invested everything he owned, even his beautiful home and assets, into this business venture. He had to stay afloat, so he had little time for anything other than pursuing his business goals. His marriage was falling apart. His children were often distant. His friends had more or less deserted him for he wasn't a pleasurable person to be around these days. In all respects my friend had fallen off the deep end and could not find his way back.

I took my friend back into time when he and his wife were first married. In fact, I was the minister who performed the ceremony some twenty years before. We talked about their new found love and happiness and how their two worlds had come together and had found meaning, peace and accord. He began to sob relentlessly as I continued talking. It was therapeutic healing.

Their lives were much simpler back then. They actually had time for one another and had spent countless hours in the mountains on weekend treks, just the two of them, in a small tent. I thought then of how happy they were and how contented they seemed to be.

Then the children came along, three of them altogether, and they began to build their world around those children. I remembered the times of baptism in the various churches I served when they would bring them to me for this family act of consecration and commitment.

But then curve balls started coming and his life took a turn for the worse when he ventured much further into his work than he had time for. He tried to accomplish too much, too fast! He was suffering from burn-out. He couldn't seem to find the peace which had recently eluded him. Now he was desperate. His wife had threatened to leave him and return to their hometown unless he got himself together again. His children had grown up basically without a father there to witness their ball games, dance recitals, or school plays.

I then asked my friend if he was ready for a change. With tears streaming down his face, he shook his head, signifying his desire. I asked him to follow me into the sanctuary where we both knelt at the altar. There I reminded him of the abundant and forgiving grace of our Lord Jesus Christ and how much Jesus loved him. I shared the story of the cross and its full implications for his life. As I recited John 3:16, my friend immediately joined me. I began praying the sinner's prayer, and soon my friend began praying it with me. We asked God to cleanse his heart and to reunite him in the love of Christ.

To make a long story short, my friend made a new commitment of his life to Christ that day and realized that what he was actually missing was the love, fellowship and direction of Christ. When he began to set new priorities for serving others instead of himself, his life began to blossom and grow beyond measure! Would that I could have 50 committed Christians like my friend in my pastorate! We could literally change the world for Christ!

Today my friend is on cloud nine with his wife, children and his church. He regularly volunteers for two-week mission trips with his church whenever he can. He is lay leader of his congregation and speaks in the pulpit when his pastor has to be on leave. What a change was wrought in his life when he placed Christ at the center once again and began serving others. His business has also been booming but he now spends less time with it and more time in service to Christ and family.

John Donne put it succinctly, *"No man is an island, entire of itself . . ."* We are not on this planet alone, but are integral parts of one another. We are *community*.

I have a friend who travels three hours one-way every two weeks to Emory University Hospital in Atlanta, Georgia, to give platelets from his blood for cancer patients who are struggling to survive. He has to lie absolutely still for two hours during the harvesting process while needles are inserted into each arm. Although he has only met a small number of the patients who have received his platelets, he feels a great sense of fulfillment and self-worth by reaching out to others in this way, . That doesn't matter, however, for my friend knows that he is doing something to help others through his small donations.

Another friend volunteers her evening hours, from 6:00 p.m. until 10:00 p.m., at her local hospital as a Pink

Lady. She'll change bed pans, deliver new linens, roll patients in wheelchairs for tests in the lab, sit beside the bed of dying patients and hold their hands . . . She would never be considered "selfish" in her quest to be of service to others! She does it six days per week after her day job. Amazing!

And then there's Johnny. Johnny spends every Saturday on a work team helping to build Habitat for Humanity houses across the southeast. He gets no monetary pay for doing this, but he tells me that the "retirement plan" is *"out-of-this-world!"*

Some years ago, I was a volunteer coordinator for the rebuilding project at Gay's Hill Baptist Church near Millen, Georgia. Gay's Hill was the first area black church to burn in a spree of arsons in the spring of 1996. Our United Methodist Volunteers in Mission took on the job of coordinating work teams from across the U.S. and Canada who were interested in helping to rebuild the burned church. The teams came from practically every state in the union and from Canada and would spend several days and even weeks in the rebuilding process. The majority of the workers and teams were Caucasian, helping to rebuild a "black" Baptist Church. Gay's Hill was to serve as the pilot project for all national church rebuilding efforts. I was there for the final touches and the dedication service, and it was certainly a time of rejoicing for all.

There was Fred and Doris Doty, a retired couple from Benton, Kentucky, who volunteered to live in a camper at a local state park. They were to be the on-site coordinators of the rebuilding each day. They were with us from the inception to the very end. Many lives were touched by this devoted and very sweet couple who felt "called" to this special ministry of care. In fact, Fred felt the call to full-time ministry while in Millen, and has served several churches before finally retiring for good. Wow, what a commitment from these two faithful servants!

Well, who ARE these people? Oddly enough, they are people just like you. They can be found in any city, on any street corner, in an elevator, or even at a social gathering. They are people who have a much higher quest in life, apart from materialism or self-gain. They have found themselves through serving others. They have ignored the old, tired routines of life, and have broken loose and given of themselves, thus finding one of the secrets of staying young and energetic.

Get in there with both feet, my friend, and become a servant to God and others. Hopefully, these examples of servant-hood will speak volumes to you and challenge you to become more and more the servant whom God is calling into action. Take those risks. Challenge the apathy in our society and make a difference. Set the example for others to follow. But don't you dare give-up or give-in! Our Lord took the form of a servant and endured the greatest of challenges when He gave His life for everyone.

The cross looms ever before us as the epitome of servant-hood. Christ took upon Himself the sins of the world and experienced the cross that you and I could receive forgiveness and establish a new relationship with Him.

If you are reading this today, God is challenging you to "the point of crisis and decision." You have this challenge before you: "Leap into faith or fall into despair." Many will perhaps turn the page at this point and decide that servant-hood is not for them. Others will perhaps embrace this concept and continue to read, searching for ways to express their faith in positive, life-affirming ways. I pray that you are in the latter category. God bless you, my friend.

Through the Valley
of the Shadow

We were in the mountains above Jericho when our tour bus pulled to the side of the road. Our guide took us up a winding little path to a small ledge where we could view the spectacular panorama below. From the ledge, we could see a monastery carved out of the mountainside. We could hear a raging stream of water far below us. A small meandering foot-trail could be seen in front of the monastery and our tour guide informed us that it was the Jericho Road. This was the road which ran down from Jerusalem to Jericho, and the actual road Jesus traveled often in His journeys.

Some distance from the monastery was a rock overhang which completely covered the path. One could not go around it but had to crouch down in order to pass beneath it to the other side. Our guide informed us that the area of the overhang had been known as "The Valley of the Shadow" for thousands of years. This was the area popularized by the Psalmist David in that beautiful twenty-third Psalm: "Yea, though I walk through the valley of the shadow of death, I will fear no evil, for thou art with me."

The Psalm now took on new life and meaning for me.

Now I knew what David was referring to in that beautiful Psalm. You and I have to pass *through* "The Valley of the Shadow" often in our lives. We can only go through alone, for there is no room for two. However, David's implication is that God goes through the valley with us!

This area was sometimes a very dangerous, treacherous place where highwaymen would often lie in wait to apprehend and steal from passersby. For me, the implication of David is that we should not fear such when passing through the valley, but stay focused on our Lord who will lead us safely through.

You may be facing surgery today or tomorrow, some overwhelming hospital procedure, chemotherapy, or even death. In the light of this beautiful Psalm, take your comfort today in knowing our Savior will go with you through every shadow of life, and He will bring you safely and lovingly to the other side. Call upon Him and He will comfort your Spirit in this hour. God bless you, my friend.

Mama's Flowers

My mother was a horticulturalist, although she never attended college or took a class in the care and management of flowers, shrubs, etc. She was well known in Helena, Georgia, as the woman with the beautiful yard and flowers. We had no grass in the yard when I was young for my mother insisted that I weed the grass out every day. She did not want it encroaching upon her flower beds. I detested that task but learned a lot from doing it which has served me well for years.

While helping mama with her flowers, I learned a lot about the different varieties and when they were expected to bloom. She taught me about the various types of fertilizer it would take for each flower to produce the most blooms. Needless to say, my mother's flower gardens became the showcase of our neighborhood for years. Other ladies were coming by regularly wanting seeds or clippings from mama's flowers. I took great pride in being a small part of her success and, to this day, I eagerly await spring in order to get my hands back into the soil!

Some people "watch" flowers grow while others are busy taking care of them so they will flourish in beauty. Life is filled with "watchers" and "workers."

Jack Taylor, My Friend

My dear friend, Jack Taylor and I have known each other for a number of years and have remained very close. Jack and I were roommates at Emory University in Atlanta, Georgia, and would talk ourselves to sleep practically every night, debating various issues. Jack is a great history buff and would begin a conversation from a very scholarly, learned point of view, and he could always rely on my down-to-earth, backwoods, realist point of view in contrast. We solved millions of problems in those conversations but the world has yet to discover them!

One night our conversation became so intense that we never could fall asleep, so we finally got out of bed, dressed, and started driving around the streets of Atlanta at two o'clock in the morning. We wound up on the northside at a Waffle House restaurant and finished off our conversation over breakfast before returning to Emory for classes. I still cherish those "great debates" and special times with my dear friend and have found Jack to always be there always for me whenever I need someone.

Jack and I still call each other to check up on our families and we'll talk a good while but we no longer get into the long-winded debates of yore. I miss that and I know Jack does as well.

Jack is finally retiring this year from *retirement*. That simply means that after his retirement, he has served a small United Methodist Church in Americus, Georgia, as a retired-supply pastor. He is finally giving that up for "real" retirement! I salute him for wanting to spend more quality time with family and friends.

Jack called a few days ago to ask me to take part in his funeral whenever he passes. He honored me with that request and I can assure Jack and you that I will not get into any of our long debates at that service, but I will share with the world my love of that guy and the great times we have had together through these many years! We're brothers in Christ, and that means a lot in this crazy, hectic-paced world today. No one can ever take that away from us. I'll always cherish his friendship, his concern, and his care. God bless you, Jack.

Cuba—From a New Perspective

I have been on three separate work teams to the island of Cuba and have had my eyes opened on each trip. For years I had grown up with the bad image of that country and its people mainly because of Fidel Castro, their dictator. While there, however, each time I would discover the Cubans to be sweet, loving, kind and considerate. They have been greatly oppressed but have continued eeking out a daily living as best they can, given their living conditions.

Each of our teams was invited to Cuba by the Methodist Church there. Castro's mother was Methodist and actually impressed upon her son to construct a statue of Christ and have it placed near the main harbor entrance to the capital city of Havana. Castro will not allow new churches to be built but will allow teams to come in and to help restore the old buildings that exist. In the process, we were able to evangelize the people by holding cell meetings wherever people would gather in various communities.

On one particular trip, we worshipped with the people of four different communities and I can truthfully say that a Revival is spreading across Cuba like wildfire! Churches are meeting under porches, in backyards, under various types of canopies—wherever they can find a place to worship. The spirit among the parishioners is tremendous and real. Lives are being changed across the island. I was particularly amazed at the zeal and excitement displayed in each worship service. I would only hope that this Revival continues to serve and transform the entire country, including the government.

In talking with one young Cuban lady, I discovered that one of her goals was to become a missionary and travel to the United States to share the gospel of Christ! Isn't that a bit interesting, especially in light of the claims that America is the most religious nation on earth? This young lady has heard, through various means, that America is in need of evangelism. I shared her concerns and agreed that a great many Americans were "religious" but lost. The fields are ready to harvest and I will pray that one day she will be able to follow her dream to America. Please pray for Cuba AND for America.

A "Grand Canyon" Experience

In 1988, my wife and I took our two small children on a vacation across the U.S. from Georgia to the Grand Canyon in Arizona. Our son Jonathan was eight and our daughter Angela was twelve. It was amazing to see, for the first time, this marvelous work of nature, carved out over thousands of years to form a mile-deep canyon in the earth.

After a day of sightseeing, the children and I decided to take the hike down the Bright Angel Trail to the Colorado River below, following the trail that pack mules have traveled for many years. A park ranger told us that we could make it down and back up in around 4-5 hours, so we decided to do it the following morning. Renee, my wife, decided to stay at the motel and read while we took our "little" trek.

With three bags of Sugar Daddies and a canteen of water, we began our journey at 8:00 a.m. It was fairly easy hiking down to the river, but devastating when coming back up!

While down on the plateau, our daughter encountered a large multi-colored snake crossing the path in front of her and she became very frightened. I consoled her and we resumed our trek. We fed the squirrels along the way from our bags of candy and enjoyed watching them feed out of our hands.

The sight from the bottom of the canyon was simply awesome! Words cannot truly express the emotions in my heart at that time and the thankfulness I was feeling for having given my children this wonderful experience.

Then began the journey back up. We would walk twenty steps and stop—twenty steps and stop. It was almost unbearable for me but even more so for the children. It took us nearly *five* hours just to make it back up to the top—nine hours total (going both down and up again). Lightning began striking all around us about half way up, and then the rains came pouring down. I quickly went from HERO to HEEL to my children in one long and grueling afternoon!

Renee had been worried sick over us since we had not returned at the approximated time and had driven from the motel to the canyon to await our arrival. She really expressed her concern when we finally did appear. I really felt like a heel at that point and most of the joys of the trip seemed to vanish. Yet, looking back, I pray that my children will always remember that we *did it!* We hiked the

Grand Canyon and lived to tell it. How many people ever accomplish such a feat in their lives? How many ever take the challenge of doing something like that? Most of us rest comfortably in our easy chairs and read articles and look at pictures of places like the Canyon but we can always say that we actually walked the Canyon. It was a journey of a lifetime, and we are far richer for having done it.

Would I do it again? Probably, if I had someone to do it with. Nothing ventured—nothing gained has always been my motto. Getting out of one's comfort zone has always been the story of my life.

Soft Landings and Smooth Flights

I recently passed by a church which had a marquee out front with the message: **God Always Promises a Soft Landing; But He Never Promised a Smooth Flight!** That saying reminded me of a flight I was on several years ago.

We had been in the Amazon region of southern Venezuela on a mission trip and had said our goodbyes to the locals at the airport which was situated near the Columbian border. Our expected flight was to pick us up and fly us to our connection in the capital city of Caracas. It never arrived, due to inclement weather over the Andes Mountains. So our team spent the night in the airport awaiting another attempt the following morning. Finally, our flight arrived early the next morning and we flew over the Andes on our way back to Caracas. That was the worst ride of my life! The bad weather kept our 747 bouncing, tilting, dropping and swaying all over the region. Several times we dropped in altitude (suddenly) and I had this strange feeling in my gut the entire trip, but we eventually made it.

At the Caracas airport, we had missed our connecting flight to Miami, with no other scheduled flights until the following day. However, this time, the airline did put us up for the night in a local motel and we got some much needed rest.

The following morning, we were finally able to catch our flight to Miami, tired, late, and very weary. Storms were all over the Miami area, so we had to circle the airport for about 45 minutes before we were able to land. Lightning was striking everywhere!

Following our Miami arrival, we learned that our next flight on one of those "puddle jumpers" had been delayed due to the weather. It would push our departure time to Tallahassee, Florida, to 7:30 p.m. Finally, we were given the O.K. to board our little American Airlines "puddle jumper" and would have to fly to Tampa, to Jacksonville, and then across to Tallahassee due to the weather. I really wasn't sure that we were going to make it home again. We were bounced around several times by the extreme weather across Florida during those two flights. We all prayed during that trip, and the Lord saw us through.

With heavy lightning and dark clouds, we finally made our approach to the Tallahassee airport. I kept looking out my window seat for runway lights in the dark, but none were visible. Finally, I could see the ground, but just before touchdown the pilot pulled the plane back up and ascended. His voice came over the intercom telling us that a light had lit-up on his console and he was told by the control tower to take it back up and circle around to check it out; something to do with the landing gear! Oh, my God! Would this trip ever end? We were tired, we were weary, and we had done a great service in missions, so please, God, help us to land this plane safely.

At that point, while the plane circled back around for another landing, I asked the twenty or so passengers (twelve were team-members) to join hands and allow me to say a prayer. As I prayed, the pilot softly landed our plane without any further complications.

Goes to show that even a mission team, doing the Lord's great work, has to go through some bumpy rides occasionally to accomplish what needs to be done. None of us are immune to such events but we can always rest in the knowledge that we are never alone in the journey. God's Word promises that he will always be with us and there will be a soft landing. Keep the faith, my friend.

God's Abundant Care

Our two fledging Carolina wrens left their nest on our back porch today. With a quick little flutter of their wings, they were off, hovering just above the ground as I watched. The mother wren stayed a close distance, watching their every move. Can it be possible that only a few days ago I had watched these two break through their tiny shells? And now, with full feathers, they were off into the big world to fend for themselves! So quickly it happened and now they are gone.

How comparable our lives are to those wrens. Yet, they never had formative years of training and growth that we experience before leaving the confines of home and family. They are on their own to face every danger and peril the world holds in store. By instinct they move about and find their way. Many will not survive their first few days because of countless predators. They will be vulnerable to every danger, yet, God protects them, according to His Word.

So much more does God care for us, my friend! Isn't that a beautiful and comforting thought? Just to know that He is there for us whenever we are in danger, whenever we leave home for the big world out there, whenever we take flight for realms beyond. He is our Creator, our Master, our King!

Just today, the first day of winter, I watched from my back porch as two young wrens fed from our bird-feeder. Could it be the same two, I wondered? I'll keep my eyes wide-open next spring to see if perhaps one of them will return and build a nest in the box on our back porch. The cycle of life will then continue, as usual. God bless.

Troglodytes troglodytes

Going Where The Fish Are

One of my elderly members in a former pastorate took me fishing one day and taught me a very valuable lesson in preparation. I decided to swing by Walmart the day before and stocked up on lures, line and other tackle for the trip, wanting to show my friend how prepared I was with all of the latest gizmos. To my surprise, he opened his tackle box and only had two lures in it, both appearing to be very old and well-used. He wasn't impressed at all with my box full of shiny new lures and the apparent price that I had paid for them.

Once we launched his John boat into the lake, he maneuvered it to a small cove and dropped anchor. I cast my line and started reeling in. Nothing. Not one single strike after many casts! I turned to my friend and said that it was about time to move elsewhere, when, all of sudden, he hung a huge largemouth bass and reeled him in. He must have been nearly five-pounds! I was excited now, and so I cast numerous other times in all directions with no luck.

Within moments, he had hung another "hog" which was bigger than the first one. I was really getting a bit irritated when he turned to me and asked if I would like to use his other lure. "Sure!" I said, and immediately put it

on my line. Then he told me where to cast and how to reel
in my line. "Be patient!" he whispered. I was beginning to
feel a bit humiliated by his remarks since I have been fish-
ing all my life!

Half way through the very first cast and reel a big
bass struck! I immediately jerked the line to set the hook,
but I lost him. My friend insisted on my being patient
again and allowing the fish a little more play time.

Moments later, I hung another one and followed my
friend's advice. After reeling in my "monster" and kissing
the fish on the head, I released him back into the lake and
thanked my friend for his timely advice and for loaning
me his lure.

Before the day ended, I had caught seven bass using
only that old borrowed wooden lure and by utilizing his
timely and simple lessons. We never once moved out of
that cove the entire trip!

I guess it boils down to this: location, knowing where
the fish are, what to use in catching them, and then how to
bring them in once you've hung them. My old friend
knew exactly where the fish would be and what it would
take to catch them through years of experience. Prepara-
tion and patience always pays a dividend.

Jesus once called to his disciples to follow him and he

would make them "fishers of men." To lead people to the Savior, one must prepare and be patient, persevere through it all until the right bait is used to lure that soul into the kingdom. It doesn't take a rocket scientist to learn how to catch bass and it doesn't take all of the latest fads and frills to lure a lost world to Christ. It only takes plain, common sense, and the willingness to go where the fish are!

Feeding the "Dump" People

I was in Nicaragua a few years ago on a whirlwind exploratory trip with Volunteers in Mission. Our goal was to set up sites and projects for future work teams. While in Leon, we visited the city dump and witnessed a local Methodist Church feeding a multitude of people who literally live there. They are referred to as the "Dump People." There are approximately 250 people living there and they spend their days collecting bottles, cans, plastic, etc. and selling these items to provide a living for their families. We stood there in the midst of this huge dump, underneath shade trees at lunchtime, and listened to the local Methodist pastor deliver a sermon to the people who had gathered for the meal. They received both spiritual and physical food that day.

The local Methodist Church in Leon prepares and provides a meal to these people five days per week through the help of our United Methodist Committee on Relief (UMCOR). Such funding is provided through our local United Methodist churches back in the U.S. through apportionment funds. It costs only $50 per week (U.S.) to feed 250 people at the dump, and I can vouch for it being well worth the effort. What a wonderful ministry to such needy people.

During the closing prayer, following the sermon, one lady from the dump asked to pray and she thanked God for our team's presence which gave them renewed hope in the midst of their overwhelming plight. She prayed that, without us and the generous gifts from UMCOR, they would be unable to survive. What a powerful prayer!

That is what's happening in one small corner of the world through the help and aid of various organizations and your generosity whenever the offering plates are passed on Sunday. The next time you place that money or check into the plate, picture these poor, indigent people of Nicaragua who send a word of "thanks" to you for caring.

"There, but for the grace of God, go you and I."

Death As An Honored Friend

And now that death on winged flight,
hath come to claim its own,
I'll leave this world on wings of joy
and sing the Seraph's song!
When you have closed my eyes in peace,
my entrance has begun;
I will not grieve in leaving here
for I shall greet the Son!

I've sought to live life borrowed
as a treasured gift so rare;
And through each day I've honored it
by showing love and care.
So when my flight that beckons
calls me gently now away,
Do not fear my leaving, dear,
rejoice with me today!

This cold and sullen body
is but the shell of mortal man;
Returning now unto the earth—
the clay, the spittle, sand.
The spirit thus, will still live on
throughout eternity.
Death has come as honored friend
and set this pilgrim free!

So when you meet my parting,
let your spirit soar above
All mortal thoughts of grieving,
let your heart be filled with love.
For soon I shall dock this destined ship
upon another shore;
Arrive at home in heaven where
I'll dwell forever more!

Milltown Closing

Milltown closed today when
the last limo of the echelon
pulled out in ranked-file and hit the road.
The stack-pipes no longer bellow their soot.
The dinner whistle was silent today,
a respite from forty-two years of labor and toil.
The limo moved cautiously down
the ragged streets of Milltown,
Slowly, as if in a funeral procession,
past rows of weather-beaten, clapboarded houses
that gave life to many families through the years;
families dependent on the wool and yarn for life.

Milltown closed today,
and all of the old men with injured hands and backs,
all of the little old ladies, broken from the weaves
and looms of the mill,
all of the dirty-faced little children—
Watched from their broken-paned windows,
from their front-porch stoops,
their backyard clotheslines—
And saw their hopes and dreams
drive away
In a long, black, shiny limousine!

Milltown closed today,
And so has my heart!

Old Spice

Isn't it funny how a smell
can conjure up so many memories?
To this day, I keep a bottle always handy,
for when I open it to smell,
I am transcended in time and space,
back to sweet memories of years now past.
I can see his rugged face,
weather-beaten by the storms of life;
hard at work down at the mill
bagging feed for the farmers.
I see his tawdry and wrinkled hands,
see his smiling face
and remember Dad!
I can see him in the fields
behind an old mule with
plow-reins in his hands
whipping them and carving out
a living from the good earth.
Oh, that sweet indescribable smell
of freshly turned earth!
And then I remember those long,
sultry summer evenings
sitting on the front porch
after an evening meal and
counting the stars and listening
to his endless stories.
All seemed well for a moment
hung in time and eternity.
Strange, isn't it,
what a bottle of *Old Spice* can
do to one's senses!

No Way to Go!

(Especially for my brother-in-law,
Monroe Shepherd)

Rows need plowing, weeds up high;
Tall grass growing on up to the sky!
Choking out life from the roots below—
Dying in the field ain't no way to go!

Daddy went down 'bout a month ago,
Breaking his back with the weeds and hoe.
Just ain't no life in this Georgia ground;
It draws life from you, then it breaks you down.

Heard 'bout a job up Atlanta way—
Maybe I'll move up there someday.
Pay out my bills, if I don't die first;
Start a new life just like a new birth.

Course, I'm a big dreamer, most farmer's are—
Hanging their hopes on the nearest star!
Living out life strugglin' day by day—
Looking at the fields just wasting away.

You know I'm kinda like that field out there,
Growing in the same place—going nowhere.
Pulling up dreams and then puttin' 'em back down—
My life's just a cycle that keeps goin' 'round!

It's a strange kinda man who tills the good earth,
Plants the seed and watches new birth.
Who looks down the furrows as far as he can see—
And faces his future in eternity!

Come Home, Poor Sailor!

I come not afraid of the venturing tide,
Nor the lateness of the day;
For I come as a friend to the lonely sea,
And watch as life drifts away!

Serenity, stillness, in the presence of God,
I cast my line to the sea;
And watch the reflections of the cool, evening tide
Reflecting those images of me.

Far from the noise of the everyday crowd,
The bustling and busyness of life—
I come for renewal of body and mind
In hopes of finding new life!

Woe to the drifter who drifts on life's sea,
Searching for regions unknown;
Wandering in darkness, forbidden he flees—
Further and further from home.

Come home, poor sailor, home from the sea;
Your drifting days are now o'er;
For you'll never find life in this world below,
Just the key which will unlock the door!

Two-Lane Morning

Blacktop shining from the rainy glaze,
Fog moving in with its grayish haze.
Early morn a'breaking through the Georgia pines,
The rain's soft tapping seems to soothe my mind.

Clap-boarded houses line the two-lane road,
Tobacco barns empty from their summer load.
Curled-up cats on an old back porch,
Birds and geese flying, all heading north.

Kind a quiet down here off the beaten path,
Nothing much to do, no reasons to laugh.
Just simple country living down here on the farm,
Away from the clamor of the city's harm.

Been right here most all of my days,
Going nowhere, never running away.
I'm a part of this place now for better or worse,
Sometimes it's a blessing—at others, a curse!

It's the only life that I've come to know,
Another two-lane morning getting ready to go!

Blind on the Appalachian Trail

Several years ago, while backpacking with my Boy Scout Troop on a stretch of the Appalachian Trail in north Georgia, I encountered a beautiful lady who was eighty-two years young . She walked into our camp late that evening with her guide dog at hand. We soon discovered that she was completely blind! That night, while sitting around our campfire, this beautiful and enriching person gave each of us a wonderful testimony and much inspiration as she shared her life with us.

Sarah Campbell was from a small northern Vermont town and had always loved the wild. At twenty-three Sarah had married and immediately started a family. She and her husband were together for the next fifty-six years! They had raised three children and had sent each on their way into the world. Three years ago Sarah's husband had died of heart disease and she had been left alone. Her three daughters had moved away to other states and each wanted mama to move in with them. She refused, however, and continued living alone. Some time later, Sarah's eyes went bad and she had to have surgery. One year later she was completely blind! Glaucoma had finally won the battle.

Through her local Lion's Club, she was able to go through the necessary training to receive a trained guide dog. She called him "Legion" (which means "many"), and Legion had since become her new set of eyes.

Sarah had always wanted to hike the entirety of the Appalachian Trail but her husband had not been the adventurous kind. Following his death, however, Sarah (then 79), decided to finally attempt this great feat—alone, with Legion—and now, totally blind!

For those Appalachian Trail friends out there who share the great bond and love of hiking, we know the many dangers and struggles it takes to accomplish such a feat with two good eyes! Imagine one blind doing so with a guide dog! Truly amazing!

Sarah's determination resounded through her story. Ludicrous, you might think, for a person like Sarah thinking that she could possibly maneuver such a dangerous trail for over 2,000 miles from Maine to Georgia! Yet, here she was in our camp, a mere thirty-five miles from the Trail's end, thirteen-months from her start. She had carried the dream and desire for so many years to make this journey of a lifetime and was now very close to fulfilling that dream.

In Sarah's sweet little voice that evening she en-
thralled me and the scouts for several hours around that
campfire. You could have heard the old proverbial "pin-
drop!" We were amazed at her accomplishment and her
many acts of bravery. Needless to say, our next three days
of hiking seemed much easier as we talked endlessly
about this wonderful and remarkable lady we had encoun-
tered.

Remembering Sarah and her great love and affection
for the outdoors and camping, I had little problem in keep-
ing my scouts inspired for the remainder of the journey.

That night together Sarah shared with us her favorite
Biblical scripture and told us how it had given her much
comfort while on the trail:

*"The Lord is my light and my salvation; whom shall I
fear? The Lord is the strength of my life; of whom shall I
be afraid?"*   (Psalm 27:1, King James Version)

Sarah Campbell had finally answered the call of her
heart and had ventured out in faith to do the impossible.
Her friends laughed at her when she first began talking
about her upcoming trip—but WHO'S LAUGHING
NOW?

Wrestling With God

My friend, the Rev. Jimmy Cason, recently had open heart surgery and has spent the last seven weeks recovering to the point where his doctor would allow him to return to the pulpit to preach. I was there last Sunday for his first sermon back since the surgery and he did a fantastic job! I could definitely tell that he had been through a storm and could relate with many in the congregation.

Jimmy entitled his sermon, "Matters of the Heart," and used the Old Testament character of Jacob. Jimmy shared with the congregation how Jacob had been led into the wilderness where he wrestled with God (Genesis 28:10-17 and Genesis 32:22-31). He used several points to drive home his "heart" experience at the Medical Center in Savannah, Georgia, and the ensuing weeks of recovery.

Following Jacob's bout with God (overcoming his personal guilt and his wilderness experience), God changed Jacob's name to "Israel" and stated that he would now become a blessing to many generations. However, Jacob would always have a physical impairment (scar) to remind him of that wrestling experience in the wilderness. In like fashion, Jimmy shared how he would carry the "zipper" scar on his chest for the rest of his life to remind him of his struggle, surgery, and recovery.

At some point, in each of our lives, we all must wrestle with God, which will ultimately have a lasting effect upon us—physically, mentally and spiritually. Physically, Jimmy will carry a reminder of his surgery on his chest. Mentally, he will have to deal with this "new" beginning and its aftermath. He will never be the same person again, for anyone who endures a wrestling match with God will change in certain respects. Spiritually, Jimmy's faith has been greatly enhanced and deepened by this experience. It has left him a better pastor, husband, father and grandfather. Family, friends and fellow church members helped bring Jimmy through this trying ordeal, giving him peace, consolation and support.

Some of you may be going through or facing a wrestling match with God today. You may still be in the wilderness searching for the way. Your guilt or sins may be weighing heavily upon you. Be patient, faithful, and know that God is there with you through that ordeal. He has promised never to leave you nor forsake you. Take comfort in knowing His presence as you call upon His Name. God bless.

Live—So the Preacher Can
Tell the Truth at Your Funeral!

The title for this article came from a church marquee the other day outside of Augusta, Georgia. I really liked it as it spoke volumes to me: *Live—So the Preacher Can Tell the Truth at Your Funeral.* Of course, I immediately began examining my own life for things that I wouldn't want a preacher to say about me at **my** funeral! All of us have things hidden deep within the recesses of our being which we prefer left unexposed. Thank goodness that mine are just petty in nature and wouldn't destroy me. But how about you? Are there things in your past that you would not want a preacher to share at your funeral?

It is important that you and I be honest with ourselves at this point. We need to examine our lives and rid our-selves of those things that so easily befall us. Repentance and cleansing are two of the most important aspects of this process; repent of our sins and be cleansed by the blood of Jesus.

Every new day presents us with a new beginning. Just as the dew falls in the wee, small hours of the morning, refreshing the earth again, so, we too, have a time of daily refreshing, an opportunity to make a change, to make a difference in our lives. It begins simply, this renewal, with your mind. Let's face it, most of our past is changeless. In most instances we cannot "un-do" what has been done but we can *reconcile* the past with those we have wronged. Forgiveness is a universal expression. Seek forgiveness from those who have been wronged. Reciprocate, if necessary. Right the wrongs of the past as best you can and then get on with the main matter of living your daily life in such a way that your pastor will have only "good" things to say about you. Strengthen the ties that bind, not just for selfish ends, but for your psychological, spiritual and physical well-being.

I always taught our two children to treat people kindly each day for one never knows when that very person will be the one who stops to help us somewhere along the road of life. Being a "heel" and always treating people with little respect or care may just leave you stranded one night along a very dark and less-traveled road!

Everything in life is relative. We are all dependent upon each other at some place or time. Treat people as you desire to be treated and they will reciprocate. You'll find your cache of friends also increasing in the process.

This process of reconciling the past is like cleaning up your own backyard before your company arrives. You wouldn't want your company to see how unkempt you are, no more than you would want a minister to lie about you at your funeral!

We are well on the road to recovery when we have taken steps to reconcile the past. If we insist on dragging the past along with us into the future we will surely be most miserable, filled with guilt and shame, and unable to live life to its fullest. Rid yourself of the ugly ogres in your past by reconciling with them today. Once you have done all that you can do, then press forward toward your goals. Change the way that you treat others, renew those broken relationships, clean up your backyard and KEEP IT THAT WAY.

Of course, this is only one small step—but a most important one. In following this step, you'll learn to like yourself all over again. Have fun in the process and gain respect along the way. Don't you dare give up, whatever you do!

Living With Birth Pangs

What does your future hold in store? What will happen to you this year, next year, ten years from now? In a sense, you have some control over much of what will happen. You are the decision-maker in your life and you will decide what will or will not occur. However, there are certain elements which are beyond our control. We cannot predict if and when these elements will occur but can only be sure that we are prepared whenever they do.

One of the many givens in life is that women will have pain in childbirth. Another is that if you live long enough and become old enough, you're going to experience some aches and pains along the way.

I play the guitar, along with several other instruments, but the guitar is my favorite. I have entertained folks with my guitar since the age of thirteen when I first learned the art and applied my skills playing with a local rock band. I have since played for countless individuals and groups in church settings to dance halls, from France and Spain to Ecuador, South America. Today, at 59, it is becoming more and more difficult for me to play the guitar because arthritis is beginning to take its toll on my fingers. My two "pinkies" are already starting to turn and curl inward and some mornings the aches and pain in those fingers are almost unbearable. Yet, I press on with every opportunity that avails itself for I know that one day I will probably be unable to play any longer. It is important that I not give up or give in to the arthritis. If I do, within a short period of time, it will eventually conquer both of my hands. I *must* keep playing! I *must* keep performing in order to exercise those fingers and keep them as flexible as possible. I simply have to interpret the arthritis as mere *birth pangs* in the progress of my life.

My feet are usually sore now each morning as I awaken. I have a middle-age spread that continues to increase in size. My hands give out earlier now whenever I'm writing or typing, although my brain wants to keep writing at a more voracious pace than ever! I have much more to say now than I had thirty years ago but why won't my body cooperate?

The simple fact of the matter is that if we continue to age, we're going to experience such *birth pangs* along the way. As one self-proclaimed prophet has put it, *"You can't even get out of this world alive! You **have** to die first!"* What a sad but true commentary. We all must die. Hopefully, however, our death won't be a painful event, although we're not given that guarantee.

We must come to terms with our birth pangs. From one stage of life to the next we will experience certain pains which accompany age and change. Change, after all, is the ultimate culprit here. But change we must if we are to survive. I much prefer the arthritic fingers than the alternative—not being able to play at all.

Change is never easy. I like the story of the snail who was traveling down the road one day and was run over by a turtle! Soon the ambulance arrived and one of the paramedics asked the snail, "What happened, Snail?" Quick came his reply, "I just don't know. It all happened so fast!"

In building your job, family, or your life, you must realize that changes are going to occur, pain will come. Suddenly, in the twinkle of an eye, things can and will happen which can change everything in your safe little world. You must prepare and be ready for those unexpected changes in order to stay ahead of the game.

A friend of mine was recently fired from his job, cold turkey! Without any forewarning, he was let go after 36 years with this particular company. He had been faithful, loyal and dedicated to his work, but they told him that day that they simply had to let someone go in order for the company to survive. How devastating this was for my friend! What is a 58 year old going to do now? Who's going to be willing to hire someone that age and for how long?

It can happen to any of us. As we move confidently through our daily routines there is always that slight possibility that something could happen to completely change the course of our comfortable little lives. What would we do then?

It is always sad whenever we hear of an employee like my friend losing his job. Perhaps if he had paid more attention to the writing on the wall he would have been preparing for that moment by checking out other job possibilities, more training, security. We are, after all, captains of our own ship!

Everyone has his own little "comfort zone" in life. We feel safe and secure whenever we're in that zone and we do not like it when people invade it. We fear any change and we become very anxious and worried whenever it is threatened. However, if we're honest with ourselves, we have to realize that sooner or later change is inevitable. It *will* come! It *will* happen! Are you prepared for it? That's the most important question.

My brother was a very good house painter for over 40 years. He has been painting houses since I was in my mid-teens. Recently, however, Robert fell from a tall ladder and broke several bones, including a few facial bones, and has been unable to recover from that event and return to work on a permanent basis. He and his wife are struggling now to meet their basic daily needs. How are they to survive? He's unable to work but does not have much saved up for this "rainy-day" in his life.

A drastic change has occurred in Robert's life and he now finds himself in unknown territory. Change has occurred and he is feeling the pressure.

Friends, change is inevitable. Birth pangs will happen if you live long enough. We must prepare for them, as best we can. Do not fear the change when it comes but see it as the possibility for opening a new area of your life yet to be explored. Move out of your comfort zone and see what life has to offer.

Be Careful What You Leave Behind

(For Melvin McBride)

Some folks leave behind their debts to others,
While others leave this world without a sign.
And some folks leave without hope for tomorrow,
While some folks leave this life with peace of mind.
Well, I hope that all is well when I depart here,
And those gates of heaven open right on time . . .

For I have always tried to pay the Piper,
And to do the things I could while I had time.
You'll find more grace in loving one another,
And living life with a satisfied mind—
So be careful what you leave behind!

Some folks leave behind their pain and sorrow,
While others try to mend their hurts with time.
And some folks try to take what life will offer,
Instead of giving back their gifts-in-kind.
Well, I hope the Master loves what they are doing,
And I pray that heaven's gates will open fine . . .

For I have always tried to pay the Piper,
And to do the things I could while I had time.
You'll find more grace in loving one another,
And living life with a satisfied mind—
So be careful what you leave behind!

A Sense of Balance

Everything in our universe exists and operates through a sense of *balance*. Our cosmos is governed by this sense, or state, and whenever it is manipulated or thrown off balance we have some form of universal calamity, such as a tsunami, hurricane, earthquake or tornado. Those tiny little mosquitoes that create havoc here in the south during our lazy, wet and humid days of summer, actually function from this sense of balance as well. Those gigantic planets in space are held in orbit on their axis as a result of balance. When we are thrown off balance, then we are in jeopardy for the forces around us bombard us without much protection.

Throughout recorded time we have always been aware that the laws of balance exist. Sir Isaac Newton stated in his *Third Law of Motion* that, *"to every action there is an equal and opposite reaction."* There are many ways to illustrate this great truth but I'll share only a few with you here.

Take a man who indulges in too much alcoholic drinking. As the alcohol takes affect upon him, he begins to stagger and weave, to become dizzy, perhaps even sick, because his body has been thrown off balance as the result of this foreign matter in his system.

If a passenger train stops all of a sudden, everything (including passengers) will rush forward in motion. When I go backpacking in the mountains, I lunge forward up those rugged slopes towards the mountaintop. My backpack is constantly pulling me backwards at the same force that I am trudging forward! Everything balances out in nature and in our universe. The law of balance works.

Another truth we should deal with at this point is one of the very fundamental laws of nature: *For every cause there is an effect.* In order to create one molecule of water, it will take two atoms of hydrogen and one atom of oxygen. In order to have electricity in our homes the combustion of fuel used to produce that electricity is essential. Always, the account balances perfectly!

A friend shared with me once that in nature there is no profit and loss account. Everything, he said, in nature balances. Although I am not a Charles Darwin fan, his theory of a *Natural Selection* process in nature warrants merit. In his theory, Darwin talks about wild creatures and their vulnerability at occasionally losing their sense of balance. If an animal becomes impaired in any fashion, that animal can usually expect a quick death, for in nature there is always another creature lurking, waiting to attack and to consume. This is not cruelty but the ways of the wild. It is nature viewed in its balancing act. Everything balances.

At this point, let's also consider some "spiritual" matters in reference to this theory of nature and our universe. You will notice that one cannot talk about **Heaven** without also inferring that there is a **Hell**. If we preach about **love**, then certainly the opposite element of **hate** exists. For every person who believes in **faith** there is an opposite of **unbelief**. One's **hope** is often balanced by **despair**. Our **courage** is balanced by **fear**.

Finally, on this point, think about one's own **immortality** (the hope of living beyond death and the grave in another realm). If we believe in our own immortality, then certainly there is the balance which exists as **mortality**.

There is also a perceived *"Law of Balance"* in the Holy Bible. God's scales of life always balance. If one sows evil he shall surely reap evil results. If one sins then surely that person will die in his sins unless he has received forgiveness. If we forgive not our brother, who has wronged us, then neither will God forgive us. If we live by the sword then we shall surely die by the sword as well! Everything balances, even in God's laws.

The purpose of this discourse has been to share with you the great importance of balance in your own personal life. You can actually learn to master that balance with purposeful living.

I love the illustration of a tight-rope walker. Suppose that a tight-rope walker lost his firm grip of the pole that keeps him balanced upon the wire? How long would it take for him to lose balance and topple to his death below? All tight-rope walkers have an unwritten law among themselves which basically reminds them to *"push their fingerprints into the pole"* while upon the wire, knowing that it is their life which hangs in the balance. Never let go of the pole! Never allow yourself to lose balance. The sudden results could be devastating.

From day-to-day newspapers report yet another person who has fallen from the balance beam of life. They have lost their grip on those things which are of vital importance to them. A young girl decides at fifteen that home is too structured and too rigid for her so she leaves home for the city where she hopes to find herself and begin a new life. Very shortly thereafter she finds herself surviving the harsh, cruel, and grinding life of the streets by prostituting herself, selling her soul for a loaf of bread and a place to stay, giving up her innocence in the process. She loses the balance beam of home and family.

A young man, angered with his parents, decides to leave home because of his differences of opinion. He drives his car at a high rate of speed down a back highway in anger. A deer crosses the road ahead of him. He swerves to avoid hitting the deer. Immediately, his car goes into a tail-spin. He looses control and crashes head-on into a telephone pole, and is killed! What a sad note to add as an example of how we lose balance but one which seems to repeat itself somewhere in this country practically every single day. The newspapers are full of reports of people who have lost their sense of balance and have, as a result, suffered terrible consequences.

It is most important that you and I maintain our sense of balance in all things. Everything balances. You must not lose your grip on those things of utmost importance. Do not let go of them! Keep your balance. And most importantly, KEEP GOD AT THE CENTER.

Little Red Wagons

My father, Carise Lee Cravey, was not a very profound man but he did make a statement once that has continued to have a profound influence in my life.

I had found myself in trouble one day in the fourth grade and had been sent to the principal's office. My mother, who worked in the school lunchroom, had been called down to the office. When mom discovered what I had done she called my dad at work and he left work and came to the school. I knew that I was doomed at that point! Nothing good could possibly come from that meeting of the minds. I was surrounded with no means of escape. For the first time in my young life I had to face the music and suffer the consequences of my actions.

After we had all been seated across from the principal's desk, the principal spelled out the elements of the crime. I had broken two windows with rocks from the playground during recess. This was actually the second time that week I had been called into the office for doing something wrong.

With the verdict in, my punishment was meted out. The principal gave me three heaving spanks from his wooden paddle, followed by my mother's two licks. Then my father had his turn at it. At that point, I lost count of how many licks he gave me! I finally cringed in a corner of that office, much like a trapped animal. That was when my father made his very profound statement that I'll never forget: "Son, everybody has to pull his own little red wagon in life." The look upon his face was one of sternness and resolution.

What I think my father was really trying to say that day was that I was ultimately responsible for my actions in life. Whatever I picked up or did during my life would go into that wagon and would eventually affect my life for good or bad.

My dad had used that neat little analogy because he knew I would understand the correlation. I had a little red wagon that I would pull to the city dump on occasion while rummaging through things people had discarded as trash. If I saw something interesting or of value I'd put it into my wagon and carry it home. I had put several discarded bikes together that way and had fun in the process. That wagon was my pride and joy!

After some time, my little wagon and I had amassed a huge pile of "treasures." Of course, there were always certain items of more importance to me than others, so I would be given the choice of loading up the things I could not use and taking them back to the dump.

So it is with our lives. We make choices and decisions each day that may or may not matter in the overall scheme of things, but some will. We must be careful about the things we put into our little red wagons (i.e., heart, conscience, behaviors), be it merely "junk" or actual "treasure." There may be some things in our wagon that need discarding. As we fill our wagons, much thought and care should be taken. Choices are made and those choices will help shape who we are and how our future will evolve. Ultimately, we are all responsible for those things we've picked up along the way.

It's amazing how much my father had learned from the time of that fourth grade experience until I turned fifteen!

Good Friends

Good friends of mine, who've stood by me
when all the others failed,
You've earned your rightful destiny
where all good friends shall dwell.

Without a fee, you've been true-blue
when kindness did not pay.
I'll always be indebted to
your caring, loving ways.

When others sought to criticize,
you always lifted me.
You never did so compromise
my rights or dignity!

What price for friendship should we pay?
There's not enough in gold!
For those who help us on our way
Shall one day save their souls!

Pot Liquor

The sweet essence of greens
flow through these veins
permeating each fiber
and reminding me of home
and mother—
Nineteen-sixty-one
in a clap-boarded two-bedroom
rustic home on the edge of town
lessons learned there
in the school of Hard-Knocks!
Struggling for survival,
greens grew cheaply
in our backyard garden.
Sweet essence of garden and home,
now long gone,
permeates this Pot Liquor soul!

Dear Old Epworth By-the-Sea

Blessed Epworth, grand old haven,
Special place of tranquility;
There I go for peace and respite,
Dear Old Epworth By-the-Sea.

'Neath your spreading oaks of grandeur,
There I take my rest in Thee.
I have loved thee like no other,
Dear Old Epworth By-the-Sea.

I can hear God's sweet voice calling.
I can feel your calming breeze.
I'm revived in heart and spirit,
Dear Old Epworth By-the-Sea.

A Call to Close

It is my fervent prayer that something in this small volume will help each of you along your journey through life. I am, by no means, a great writer—merely a messenger of God's grace and tender mercy. My poetry has been of great comfort to me and, thus, I pray that you will hopefully find some comfort therein as well. My books will perhaps never line the shelves of large bookstores, but if you are holding and reading one of them at this moment, my mission has been accomplished.

Know that you are loved, my friend, and that God has a special place for each of you in His glorious kingdom! Make peace with your fellow pilgrims through life and also with God. They will each bring you peace and comfort through the storms of life. Maintain balance and trust in your heart and, therein, find joy in this life. It is not a perfect world. Love it, protect it, and share it with others, for life is found in the journey, THE ROAD LESS TRAVELED, not in our final destination! Be well!

Dr. Charles E. Cravey
December 2010

For Additional Copies:

IN HIS STEPS PUBLISHING
6500 Clito Road
Statesboro, Georgia 30461

Please enclose $14.95 per book
plus $1.50 for shipping.

www.ingramcontent.com/pod-product-compliance
Lightning Source LLC
Chambersburg PA
CBHW070059260626
47160CB00004B/1254